THE BEAUTIFUL WAY OF LIFE

The Beautiful Way of Life

A Meditation on Shantideva's Bodhisattva Path

René Feusi

Wisdom Publications • Boston

Wisdom Publications
199 Elm Street
Somerville, MA 02144 USA
www.wisdompubs.org

Library of Congress Cataloging-in-Publication Data
Feusi, René, author.
 The beautiful way of life : a meditation on Shantideva's Bodhisattva path / René Feusi.
   pages cm
 ISBN 1-61429-189-6 (pbk. : alk. paper)— ISBN 978-1-61429-206-7 (Ebook)
 1. Santideva, active 7th century. Bodhicaryavatara. 2. Spiritual life--Buddhism. I. Title.
 BQ3147.F48 2015
 294.3'85--dc23

                      201402059

ISBN 9781614291893   ebook ISBN 9781614292067

19 18 17 16 15   5 4 3 2 1

Photos from Dharma Eye (dharmaeye.com): Michael Ash, pages x, 82; Olivier Adam, pages 52, 60; Victoria Knobloch, pages 6, 124; Lera Grant-Evdokimova, pages 18, 36; Tadas Juras, page 26; Risto Kuulasmaa, page 14. Cover design by Phil Pascuzzo. Interior design by Gopa&Ted2, Inc. Set in Hoefler Txt 10/14.4.

Please visit www.fscus.org.

Contents

Preface

MANY YEARS AGO, I rented a cabin in Bodh Gaya, the blessed place where the Buddha reached enlightenment, with the idea of doing a silent retreat. Soon after entering seclusion, however, work started on the erection of a new building right in front of my cabin. Construction would begin early in the morning and continue until late in the afternoon. At night, the sound of crackling loudspeakers blaring popular Indian music prevented me from sleeping, let alone remaining focused in meditation. My earlier fantasies of being close to the Bodhi tree, hearing the sweet whiffle of the wind in a pipal tree, watching a gently meandering river, or gazing on the golden tapestry of rice fields were shattered. Instead of becoming more peaceful and inspired, I found myself increasingly irritable and restless. I seriously contemplated leaving, but giving up felt like defeat.

At that moment I remembered Shantideva's *Bodhisattva Way of Life*. The classic guide to becoming a bodhisattva, one who strives for enlightenment in order to perfectly serve all beings, was one of the few books I was traveling with. It had a chapter on patience. What better opportunity than the present circumstances to put it into practice! I spent the next weeks studying the text, focusing especially on the sixth chapter. I was amazed by the effectiveness of Shantideva's clear logic. Meditating on patience gradually appeased my frustration and, to my astonishment, I was actually able to develop gratitude for the outer disturbances.

Shantideva's *Bodhisattva Way of Life* is a remarkable practice manual written in exquisite poetry. It gradually outlines the whole spectrum of mind training up to enlightenment, covering:

- An explanation of the benefits of entering the bodhisattva path
- How to prepare the mind to enter this path
- How to take the vow to become all-knowing out of altruism
- How to strengthen this resolve
- How to cultivate mindfulness in daily life
- How to gradually bring to perfection generosity, ethics, patience, perseverance, concentration, and wisdom, all necessary for reaching the goal of full enlightenment
- Concluding altruistic prayers

In Shantideva's vision, bodhisattvas may be solitary, but they never feel alone, as they continuously place themselves in the caring presence of the buddhas and the spiritual masters. They conquer their afflictive emotions and perfect their conduct with tremendous patience and perseverance. As progress unfolds they experience ever-greater peace, contentment, and compassion. They live freely in the world, driven only by their altruistic wish to benefit others.

While getting more immersed in the text and its logic, I found that the meaning was sometimes veiled in the beautiful poetry. So, as a personal exercise, I took up my pen to extract the meaning of each verse and draw out Shantideva's lines of reasoning. After finishing the chapter on patience, having enjoyed the task so much, I moved on to the other chapters.

Later, while residing at Vajrapani Institute in California, I showed the work to Fabienne Pradelle, who encouraged me and helped me to finish it, thinking it would benefit others. Working with several different translations, when verses were translated to have different meanings, I chose the one that made the most sense to me given Shantideva's line of reasoning. In many places I reduced the elaborations while keeping the essence of the meaning of each verse and retaining the same number of verses. The exception was the ninth chapter on wisdom. The content being so complex and the meaning sometimes hidden, the emphasis there was put on clarity of meaning rather than length. As a result, some of the verses ended up being longer than the original. In addition, Shantideva, a Buddhist monk, composed the text in India in the eighth century and conformed to the gender bias of the time. I did not see any benefit in maintaining that view for a Western audience in the twenty-first century. Finally, I added some headings, hoping to make the structure clearer and for ease of use—to help the reader find relevant passages. Judith Kondo then went over the whole text and brought it to its present polished language. I wish to express my sincere gratitude to both Fabienne and Judith, for without their friendly help this distilled version would never have appeared.

I am also thankful to David Kittelstrom and all those at Wisdom who contributed the final touches, including a beautiful layout and photographs that lend themselves to contemplative reading. And finally my deepest gratitude goes to all my teachers, actual examples of bodhisattvas in daily life, for without their inspiration and teachings, I wouldn't be traveling on this inner journey. Foremost among them is Kyabje Zopa Rinpoche, who has guided me patiently from the very beginning and awakened my curiosity about and appreciation for Shantideva.

This present distillation is by no means intended to be a replacement for Shantideva's work, the verse numbers of which are given alongside their corresponding lines here. In fact, I strongly recommend that everyone not only read his text many times but also receive teachings and read commentaries on it as well. Instead, this work is intended as a complementary meditation manual.

This manual can be used in many different ways: to find encouragement when one feels lazy, as advice for everyday mind training, as a preliminary to meditation or as a meditation itself, or as break-time reading on a comfortable chair with a cup of tea! It is my hope that the conciseness of this text will make the content of the masterpiece easier to integrate into one's meditation practice—and therefore, optimistically, more frequently put to use.

As Shantideva himself says at the outset of his work:

> This text contains nothing
>   that has not been said before;
> I composed it solely to train my mind.
> However, should others chance upon it,
>   it may benefit them, too.

1

The Excellence of Bodhichitta

I pay homage to the Three Jewels   1
and hereby promise to explain
    the bodhisattva's way of life.

This text contains nothing   2
    that has not been said before;
I compose it solely to train my mind.
However, should others chance upon it,   3
    it may benefit them too.

Favorable conditions are hard to find;   4   *preciousness*
if I don't take advantage of them now,   *of human life*
    when will such a chance arise again?

Good thoughts are as rare and brief   5   *karma*
    as lightning illuminating a dark night.
Negative ones are common and strong;   6
what goodness other than bodhichitta
    can vanquish them?

The buddhas saw it is bodhichitta alone 7
   that can lead beings to the greatest happiness.

bodhichitta's benefits

Whoever wishes happiness for themselves or others 8
   should keep it tightly in their hearts.

And whoever generates it, 9
   despite wandering in samsara,
will become Buddha's child, a figure to be praised by all.

Bodhichitta is the elixir that transforms this ordinary 10
   body into a buddha's form.

The buddhas recognized its great value; 11
wandering beings, likewise, should hold it firmly.

Bodhichitta alone bears fruit forever; 12
other virtues, like banana trees, bear fruit just once.

It easily purifies extremely heavy negative actions, 13
so why not rely upon it?

Like time-ending fires, 14
   it burns off, in an instant,
   enormous negative karmic forces.

Bodhichitta is of two types: 15
   aspiring to awaken
   and actually *engaging* in the method to awaken.

types of bodhichitta

The distinction between them is the same 16
   as between aspiring to go
   and actually going.

Aspiring has great benefits   17
   but is not a continuous source of merit.
With *engaging*, however, even distracted or asleep,   18
   merit continually increases.   19
Buddha explained this for those inclined to lesser aims.   20

If wishing to relieve a mere headache of another person   21   *why beneficial*
   brings immeasurable merit,
what then of wishing to eradicate suffering   22
   and bring happiness to every being?
Do even our fathers or mothers   23
   have such generous intentions?
Do the gods, sages, or even Brahma?
Even in their dreams,   24
   such a wish for themselves cannot be found,
   let alone for others!

This intention is an extraordinary jewel of mind   25
and its birth an unprecedented wonder.

It's the cause of happiness for beings,   26
   a remedy for their sufferings.
How can its qualities be measured?

If the mere *aspiration* to benefit   27
   excels venerating the buddhas,
what then to say of *engaging* to make everyone happy?

Beings strive for happiness 28
but constantly create the causes of its opposite.

For those destitute of happiness, 29
bodhichitta relieves them from countless sorrows
    and fills them with bliss;
where else could such a precious friend be found? 30

We praise one who repays kindness received; 31 *praising those*
what to say of one who gives freely? *who practice it*

If simply giving a meal is virtuous, 32
what then of bringing all beings to enlightenment? 33

Harboring negative thoughts 34
    toward such a bodhisattva
will cause lengthy rebirths in unfortunate realms.

Positive thoughts, however, will create far greater merit, 35
for even in the most acute situations,
bodhisattvas never commit negative deeds
    but only do good naturally.

I pay homage to those in whom 36
    this sacred state of mind has risen
and who benefit even their enemies.

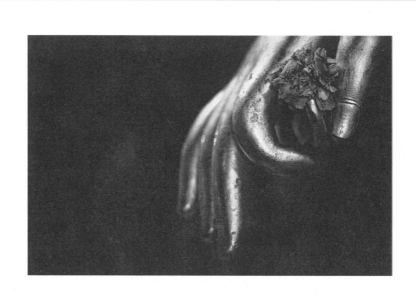

2
Confession

In order to take hold of this precious mind,   1
to the Three Jewels I sincerely offer:

Water, flowers,   2   *offering things*
fruits, and medicine,   *not owned*
mountains of jewels,   3
trees laden with blossoms and fruit,
forest groves,
perfume, incense,   4
wild harvests,
and all ornaments,
lakes and pools adorned with lotuses,   5
and the sweet-voiced calls of swans.

All these I create in my mind   6
and offer to the compassionate lords.

Destitute of merit, I have nothing else to offer.   7
Protectors, for my sake,
   please accept it all.

I offer myself to you throughout all my lives.   8   *offering oneself*
If you accept me, I will   9
   be without fear,
   go beyond the evils of my past,
   and benefit all.

In a bathing chamber with crystal floors,   10   *mentally*
   pillars of gems, and canopies of pearls,   *created*
I will bathe the buddhas and their children   11   *offerings*
   with water, sweet and fragrant.
With perfumed towels I will dry their bodies   12
   and offer scented clothes.
With excellent garments and finest jewels   13
   I will adorn them.
With sumptuous fragrance   14
   I will anoint their bodies.

Beautiful flowers strung in garlands,   15
clouds of choicest incense,   16
delicacies and nectar to drink,
precious lamps, golden lotuses,   17
incense-sprinkled grounds strewn with flower petals,

palaces resonant with songs,   18
    radiant with pearls and gems
    and jeweled parasols, I offer,   19
as well as a celestial symphony   20
    to soothe the suffering of living beings.

May a rain of flowers unceasingly stream   21
    down upon the precious Triple Gem.

Just as Manjushri and other bodhisattvas   22
    made sublime offerings,
so shall I.

With faith, esteem, and a sea of lyric praise,   23
    manifesting as many bodies   24
    as atoms of the world,
I bow down to the Three Jewels   25
    and all worthy of homage.

Until enlightenment   26   *refuge*
I go for refuge
to the Three Jewels.

I beseech you with folded hands: 27   *power of regret*

Since beginningless time,   28
I have committed harmful actions
    and caused them to be done.

In ignorance, I rejoiced in what was done;   29
now, seeing my mistake,
    I confess.

Whatever wrongs I have done   30
    toward the Triple Gem,
    my parents,
    my spiritual masters,
    and others,
I openly admit to you.   31

I may well die   32
    before having purified them all;
please protect me,
    for this fleeting life is unstable.   33

For the sake of friends and enemies   34
    I committed evil,
but leaving all
    I must depart alone.

My friends, enemies, all others,   35
    and I myself
will cease to be,
and all that I possess,   36
    like dream objects,
will be no more.

Many friends and enemies
   have passed already,
but the wrong I have done for their sake
   remains ahead of me.

37

Out of ignorance, lust, and hate,
I have committed so much negativity.

38

Never halting night or day,
my life is slipping by,
   never to be regained.
Alone I will have to go.
And then what help will be my friends?
Only goodness gained thus far
   will be of any assistance.

39

40

41

Alas, so many negative actions have I gathered
for the sake of this transient life!

42

If a man being led to torture
   is transfigured by fear,
what need to mention my misery
when stricken down
   by the frightful messenger of death?
Panic-stricken, I will then seek protection,
but nowhere will help or refuge be found.

43

44

45

46

So from this day I go for refuge to the buddhas,   47   *power of*
to the Dharma   48   *support*
and the bodhisattvas,
    to Samantabhadra and Manjushri,   49
    Avalokiteshvara,   50
    Akashagarbha, Kshitigarbha,   51
    and Vajrapani.   52
Your words I have transgressed;   53
now in terror I turn to you
    and plead protection.

Alarmed by mere common ills,   54   *power of*
    I act according to the doctor's word.   *antidotes*
So if all earthly beings can be overcome   55
    by just one of the many mental poisons
    and no other remedy can be found,
not to act according to the advice   56
    of the all-knowing Physician
would be worthy of scorn.

If along an ordinary cliff   57
    I need to tread with care,
all the more then
    near the unfathomable precipice.

Foolish it is to enjoy myself,   58
    thinking today I won't die,
for the time will surely come.

And with death approaching,   59
how can I relax
  in carefree ease?

Of life's past experiences,   60   *power of*
  what now remains?   *determination*
And if alone I must depart,   61
  what use are friends and enemies?

Surely my only concern   62
  night and day
should be to free myself from misery.

All the wrongs   63
  and transgressions of my vows
  committed out of ignorance,
with a mind terrified of the suffering to come,   64
  I humbly confess it all.

Please, guides of the world, accept me,   65
and all these evil actions
  I shall do no more.

3
Committing to Bodhichitta

With joy, I celebrate the positive actions   1   *rejoicing*
    that rescue beings from the lower realms
    and place them in better rebirths.

I rejoice in the gathering of virtue   2
    that causes liberation,
in the enlightenment of the buddhas   3
    and their spiritual children,
in the ocean of virtue   4
    that arises from generating bodhichitta,
and in actions that benefit others.

I request the buddhas   5   *requesting*
to shine the Dharma's lamp.   *buddhas to*
                                                   teach

I join my hands in beseeching you: 6   *requesting them*
Please remain among us for innumerable eons!   *to remain*

By the virtues I have thus collected,   7   *dedication*
may the sorrows of every living being be ended,
and may I serve as the doctor, the nurse,   8
    and the medicine itself
    until everyone is healed.

May I dispel hunger and thirst   9
    with a rain of food and drink,
and during eons of famine
    may I transform myself into those things.
May I become everything the poor and destitute   10
    could need
    and stay close to them.

My body, enjoyments, and all my virtues,   11   *training in*
I offer without any sense of loss;   *generosity*
nirvana is attained by giving away everything,   12
so best to give it all to others.

Having given them my body,   13
    may they use it as they please,
    merely for their happiness.   14
Having now given it away,
    why should I hold it dear?
May it be a source of benefit for all.   15

If those who see me   16
    develop an angry or unkind thought,
may that negative mind
    always turn into a cause of happiness for them.
May those who harm me reach enlightenment.   17

May I be a guide, a protector,   18
    a boat, a bridge,
    an isle, a lamp,   19
    a bed, a servant,
    a wishing jewel,   20
    a vase of plenty,
    a powerful mantra,
    a wish-granting tree, and more.

Like the earth may I be the ground   21
    and sustenance of all beings,
and till they pass to nirvana,   22
may I provide their livelihood and nourishment.

Just as the previous buddhas   23   *taking the*
    gave birth to bodhichitta   *bodhisattva*
    and then trained in the method leading to   *vow*
    enlightenment,
I will do likewise,   24
    for the benefit of all beings.

And now for this pure state of mind
   to constantly increase,
I should praise it in this way:

rejoicing in
one's own good
fortune

25

26

Today my life has given fruit,
for I have become the buddhas' child.

27

In every way, I will act
   in accordance with such a rank.
For like a blind man
   who has stumbled upon a jewel,
bodhichitta has been born within me.

28

It's the supreme ambrosia for defeating death
   and an inexhaustible treasure,
   the supreme medicine,
   the tree that shelters,
   the bridge from lower realms to happiness,
   the rising moon,
   a mighty sun,
   quintessential butter.
All you who yearn for happiness,
   it will fill you with joy.

rejoicing in
being able to
fulfill others'
wishes

29

30

31

32

33

Today, in the presence of all protectors,
I summon the world to supreme happiness.

34
calling all to
true joy

4
Attending to Bodhichitta

Having firmly gained hold of this bodhichitta,   1
I will strive never to turn away from it.

When it comes to reckless or ill-considered actions,   2   *not abandoning*
   changing one's mind makes sense,   *bodhichitta*
but how could I ever withdraw   3
   from what has been so thoroughly examined
   by the buddhas and myself?

If after having promised, I fail to act   4
   and thus betray all beings,
   what kind of rebirth will I take?
If withdrawing from even a modest generous intention   5
   leads to rebirth as a hungry ghost,
then if I break my promise to all beings,   6
   how will I ever gain a happy rebirth?
Only the omniscient can see how those   7
   who give up bodhichitta
   nonetheless reach liberation.

This failure is the gravest of all downfalls,   8
as the good of all beings is discarded.
Likewise, anyone who hinders   9
     the deeds of a bodhisattva
     will wander endlessly in despair.
If destroying a single being's joy will ruin me,   10
     what then to say of thwarting the happiness of all?

Those who generate bodhichitta but later give it up   11
will long be excluded from the higher spiritual levels.
Therefore, I resolve to act   12
     according to the promise I have made.

Countless buddhas have come and gone,   13   *abandoning*
yet because of my faults   *nonvirtue*
     I was not saved by them;
and if I continue like this,   14
again and again I will suffer more pain
     and bondage.

The advent of a buddha,   15
     being human,
     and having faith,
all these are rare;
     when will they be found again?

Today, I am healthy   16
     with means of livelihood,
yet life is slipping by.

Currently I act in such a way   17
    that I will not regain this human form;
losing it,
    my bad actions will be many.
For if I am not virtuous while human,   18
how will I act when tormented
    by the misery of lower realms?

Amassing countless nonvirtues,   19
for eons I will not find a happy life again.
To illustrate this, the Buddha gave us   20
    the example of the turtle in the sea.

If an instant's fault   21   *cultivating*
    can lead me downward for eons,   *virtue*
how many causes of rebirth in hell have I created
    since beginningless time?
But experiencing that pain won't free me either,   22
for in such states I will create
    much more negative karma.

So if, having found leisure such as this,   23
    I do not train in virtue,
what greater folly could there be?
Having understood this,   24
    if I still waste my time,
death will bring great regret,
and in the sufferings of lower realms,   25
    I will be plagued by infinite remorse.

Having found this precious opportunity,   26
if I am led to hell again,
then, as though under a spell,   27
   my will is thwarted.
What *is* this spell that so confounds me?

Anger and attachment are neither courageous   28   *the faults*
   nor wise;   *of mental*
how have I become their slave?   *afflictions*
It's I who welcome them into my heart   29
and passively allow their harm.

Were all beings to rise up as my enemies,   30
   even they could not lead me to hell,
but these mental afflictions can, in an instant,   31
   cast me into those flames.

No other enemy indeed has lived as long as they.   32

Pleasing other enemies turns them into friends,   33
but pleasing mental afflictions
   only makes them worse.

How can I be joyful,   34
   with these enemies lodging at ease
   within my heart?
What happiness can ever be my destiny?   35

Therefore, I won't abandon the fight   36
until these enemies of mine are slain.

If men can endure many wounds   37   *rising to the*
   for the sake of meaningless battle,   *challenge*
then needless to say that I, regardless of the hardship,   38
   will work to overcome the source of all my pain.

Wounds are any soldier's trophy,   39
so why, in this high endeavor,
   should pain dismay me?

When for the sake of livelihood alone,   40
   people endure so much hardship,
why can't I put up with adversities?

When I pledged to free all from the delusions,   41
I was not yet freed from mine,
so this was clear insanity;   42
all the more reason never to give it up!

This will be my sole obsession,   43
and I will use even the mental afflictions themselves
   to destroy this enemy!
Better to die   44
   than to ever bow down to these afflictions.

Common enemies, when defeated,   45
simply retreat and regain strength,
but delusions chased away by wisdom   46
   are without such strategies.
Why then am I so lazy?

Mental afflictions aren't found in the object,   47
   nor in the subject;
     they are simply mirages.
Therefore take heart!
Why needlessly suffer so?

Having pondered like this,   48
I will apply myself to the training.
If the doctor's instruction is ignored,
   how will the patient be cured?

5
Mindfulness

Without guarding the mind attentively   1
  guarding one's practice is impossible.
Even a crazed elephant can't cause as much harm   2
  as an untamed mind.
But for a mind bound with mindfulness,   3
  everything becomes possible.
Wild animals, spirits, enemies—   4
all will be tamed by having tamed this mind.   5

All the suffering there is,   6
  up to the worst suffering of the hells,   7
originates from the untamed mind.   8
Nothing is more dangerous.

As poverty still exists,   9   *the perfections*
  how is giving perfected?   *as expressions of*
Through a mind with the sheer wish   10 *the tamed mind*
  to give everything.

Animals are still being killed,   11
but the mind that gives up such acts
   is considered ethically perfect.

Enemies are too numerous to destroy,   12
but abandoning anger achieves the same purpose.

I cannot cover the planet with leather,   13
but I can cover my feet.
Likewise, I am unable to control external events,   14
but if I tame my mind,
   what else needs to be controlled?

Speech and action don't achieve the results   15
   achieved by a subdued mind;
prayer and meditation are futile   16
   if practiced with a distracted mind.
Thus those who seek happiness   17
   without understanding the mind
   work in vain.

Therefore, I must tame my mind;   18   *taming through*
without this, what use are many other trainings?   *effort*

Living amid difficult people,   19
like a wounded one I should protect my mind.
For if I protect a common wound,   20
why not protect a wounded mind
   for fear of hell?

If I always remain so diligent, 21
then neither attractive nor harmful people
    will unsettle my mind.
Though my fame, fortune, or other virtues fade, 22
never will I let my mind degenerate!

O you who wish to guard your mind, 23
I pray that you always be mindful and introspective.

taming through mindfulness and introspection

Like a sick man drained of strength, 24
the scattered mind accomplishes little,
and like a leak in a jar, 25
lack of introspection prevents
    what has been heard, pondered, and meditated upon
    from being retained in memory.

Many otherwise devoted and learned 26
commit downfalls from lack of mindfulness.
To steal our merit 27
    and send us to lower realms,
the thieves of distraction and delusion 28
    lie in wait for a breach in mindfulness.
I will practice mindfulness at all times, 29
and if momentarily lost,
    restore it by recalling the hells.

Surrounded by masters,   30
    practicing with respect,
mindfulness develops easily.

Buddhas see everything, including me,   31
so with respect I should remember their presence.   32

When introspection is set to guard the mind,   33
mindfulness will come and,
    even when lost, be regained.

First I should check my mind   34   *ethic of*
and, if a delusion is present,   *restraint*
    refrain from action.

I will not let my gaze wander aimlessly   35
but will always look down
    as in meditation.
However, to rest for a while,   36
I may look around and greet those I see.
Walking, I may sometimes stop   37
    and check around me for any danger   38
and then proceed accordingly.

If I decide "my body should act like this,"   39
I should periodically check to see that it does so.
Likewise, I should watch my mind to ensure   40
    it remains bound to the pillar of Dharma.

In this way, I will never,   41
   not even for an instant,
   let go of the investigation
   of my mind's movements.
But if I'm unable, when in danger or celebration,   42
I'll let it do what's appropriate.

Having begun something,   43
I'll think of nothing else until it's accomplished.
In this way, all is done well;   44
else nothing is achieved,
   and I become confused.

All interest in gossip and entertainment,   45
   on which too much time is spent,
as well as any meaningless action,   46
I should abandon.

Before performing any action of body or speech,   47
I should first check my mind:
If I find attraction or aversion,   48
if it's under the power   49
   of arrogance, pride, or jealousy,   50
if it pursues material gain, honor, or praise   51
   or seeks my interest over others',   52
if it's timid or impudent, impatient, or lazy—   53
in any of these cases,
   I'll be like a log.

Whenever my mind is disturbed in these ways,   54
I'll apply the antidotes.

Determined, kindhearted, stable, respectful,   55   *ethic of virtue*
    mindful of karma,
    available to help,
never disheartened by the contrary wishes   56
    of childish beings
but always compassionate toward their mental afflictions,   57
and understanding that ego, like an illusion,
    has no reality:
thus I will make my mind like a mountain,   58
constantly reflecting on the great opportunity
    of the precious human life at last attained.

O mind, why care so much for this body   59   *abandoning*
    that after death will be left behind?   *attachment*
Since this body is separate from you,   60   *to the body*
what can it do for you by itself?

Why worry about a thing so full of filth?   61
If dissected with wisdom's scalpel,   62
what essence will be found?   63
Not finding any,   64
    why protect it with such attachment?

O foolish mind, body's excrement you don't eat,   65
    nor do you drink its blood,
so what use is it to you?

One day, death will take it 66
   away from you, 67
so why pamper it so? 68

Use this body for your best interest, O mind! 69
See it as a boat that comes and goes at your will 70
   to fulfill the wishes of others.

I'll be master of my mind, smiling, 71   *training in*
   a true friend to the world.   *virtue*
Considerate of others, 72
   I'll delight in being quiet,
like cats and thieves 73
   that accomplish their aim by being discreet.
Respectfully, I'll pay attention 74
   to the skilled advice of others
and give encouragement and praise 75
   for good things done.

I'll speak of others' good qualities 76
   when they're out of sight,
and when my own are mentioned,
   think of them with appreciation.
Let me rejoice in others' 77
   good actions and happiness,
for in this life I won't lose anything, 78
   and in future ones I'll gain great happiness.

Let me speak from the heart, just enough,   79
    in a clear and pleasing way.
When I see beings, may I think: 80
    "Depending on them I shall reach buddhahood."

May I build up my character by my virtuous aim   81
    through applying the antidotes
    and through being helpful to others.
And in performing any of my actions,   82
I'll rely on no one but myself.

I'll train in the perfections gradually.   83
The latter ones being more exalted,
I will not discard a greater perfection
    for a smaller one,
and I will always consider the benefit of others.

Having realized this well,   84   *ethic of*
let me work for others with constant energy.   *benefitting*
Eating simply, let me share my food   85   *others*
    with the ordained and beggars
and be ready to sacrifice all but my robes.

This body is for the Dharma;   86
let me handle it with care.
Let me use it for the highest aim   87
and not give it away until my compassion is pure.

I won't teach the Dharma to those who lack respect,   88
I'll show equal deference toward teachings   89
   of initial and supreme aim
and teach others according to their capacity.   90

Let me be considerate of others' property,   91
eat with good manners,   92
and not sit with stretched legs or crossed arms.
I'll always abandon what's offensive to others.   93
I won't point with my finger   94
   but indicate the way with my whole hand,
nor wildly wave my arms or shout out loud,   95
   unless in urgency,
or else I'll lose control.
I'll sleep in the lion pose   96
and, with alertness, resolve to rise early.

Practices are countless,   97   *perfecting ethics*
but these that cleanse the mind
   are the most important.
Six times a day, I'll recite the *Three Heaps Sutra*   98
   and thus neutralize my downfalls.

Let me diligently apply the training   99
   appropriate for each situation,
since for a skilled bodhisattva,   100
   each moment is transformed into virtue.

I'll do all actions for others' benefit   101
and dedicate them toward enlightenment,
and I'll never, even at the cost of my life,   102
give up a guru skilled in the Mahayana.
Relating respectfully to a guru can be understood   103
   from reading the sutras,   104
and the bodhisattva trainings   105
   from the sutras and Nagarjuna's texts.   106
Let me implement fully these trainings   107
   to protect this worldly mind.

Mindfulness in brief is this: 108   *conclusion*
repeatedly checking the state of body and mind.
I must put all this into practice,   109
for what benefit is there in merely reading
   the doctor's prescription?

6
Patience

Merits painstakingly gathered   1   *faults of anger*
     over a thousand eons
will be destroyed in a flash of anger.
Therefore, there's no virtue like patience,   2
     which I must strive to cultivate.

While under the influence of anger,   3
no joy, peace, or sleep is to be found.
An angry man is in danger of being attacked,   4
     even by those who depend upon his kindness.
He will be abandoned by friends,   5
     losing happiness and peace.

Recognizing the faults of anger,   6
I must persevere in overcoming it
     in order to find peace.

Being unhappy at not getting what I want   7
    or at getting what I don't want
    is the fuel of anger.

Therefore I must destroy this unhappy mind   8
    that causes my downfall.
Whatever happens, let my joy be undisturbed,   9
for dissatisfaction is fruitless
    and destroys my virtue.

If a problem can be remedied   10
    why worry?
And if a problem can't be remedied
    what's the use of worrying?

We wish to spare our loved ones and ourselves   11   *benefits of*
    suffering and humiliation,   *enduring pain*
but for our enemies we wish the opposite!

Pleasure is hard to find and pain abounds.   12
But it's from pain that the wish for freedom arises.
So, my mind, be strong!

Some ascetics afflict themselves with great pain 13
    for mere liberation's sake,
so why am I so cowardly
    when seeking complete enlightenment?

Everything gets easier with familiarity.   14
So I'll train myself to bear first minor
   then great adversity.

Isn't this true with mosquito bites,   15
   heat and cold,
   and other small difficulties?
Being concerned only makes them worse.   16

How I experience things depends upon   17
   my state of mind,
   whether resolute or cowardly;   18
therefore I'll ignore all harm and suffering.

Pain should not disturb my peace,   19
for I should expect battling delusions to be hard.
The real heroes are those who fight this war   20
   and face pain bravely.

And pain has precious benefits: 21
   it dispels arrogance
   and fuels compassion;
   it makes me cautious of karma
   and ready to take refuge.

I don't get angry with common sicknesses,   22   *causes of anger*
   which arise without volition,
so why resent other beings whose mental afflictions   23
   arise in the same way?

People don't think, "I am going to get angry."   24
Anger doesn't think, "I will arise."   25
All negativities arise   26
    through the force of causes and conditions.   27
None are independent.   28
The assembly of causes doesn't think "I create."   29
Effects don't think "I am being created."   30
Thus everything depends on causes,   31
so why get upset at illusions?

"Then there's no point in resisting anger!"   32
Yes there is, because it cuts the stream of suffering.

When someone behaves badly,   33
remember such things arise from conditions,
    and then stay at peace.

If things happened by wishing alone,   34
then no one would suffer,   35
    for no one wishes it!
Yet carelessly, beings harm themselves   36
    in endless ways.

If through longing and obsession   37   *not retaliating*
    people will even kill themselves,
how can I expect them not to harm others?
Those victims of their own delusions;   38
even if I can't have compassion for them,
    I certainly shouldn't get angry!

If their nature is to harm others,   39
    like fire's nature is to burn,
then isn't getting irritated pointless?

And if their true nature is good,   40
    and ill deeds merely passing,
wouldn't getting angry at them be like
    resenting space for letting smoke rise?

I don't get angry at the stick,   41
so I shouldn't get angry at its wielder
    but at the anger.

I should think: "In the past, I inflicted   42
    the same thing on others,
    so this is the result of my past actions."
Both the stick and my body   43
    are the causes of my pain,
so where should I direct my anger?

I created this suffering body out of desire;   44
why get upset at its pain?

We shrink from suffering but love its causes.   45
Since this pain is self-inflicted,
    why get angry at others?
My past actions are the sole creator of my pain;   46
with whom should I get upset?

Those who persecute me are impelled   47
    by my past actions;
so they will suffer because of me.
Thanks to them I purify,   48
but thanks to me they'll suffer in hell.   49
So getting angry at them is perverse!

Controlling my anger will bring me a good rebirth,   50
but what will happen to my enemies?
If I returned pain for pain,   51
they'd still not be saved,
and my bodhichitta would be impaired.

Mind is immaterial.   52   *enduring*
If it's affected by physical pain,   *humiliation*
    it is from its attachment to the body.
Slander and abuse don't harm the body,   53
    so why get upset?

Being disliked won't kill me,   54
    so why be afraid of it?
"Because it will hinder my getting what I want!"   55
But profit will vanish with this life,
    while karma will not.
Better to die now than to live a wicked life;   56
now or then, the pain of death will be the same.

Happiness, whether long-lasting or short-lived,   57
   like a dream,   58
will be finished at death.
Though I may enjoy great wealth and pleasures,   59
in the end I'll have to go empty-handed.

And if I think with wealth   60
   I can collect merit and purify,
be careful! Grasping at wealth
   brings the opposite.
What use would this kind of harmful life be?   61

If I claim that it is right to be upset   62
   by insulting words,
why don't I get upset when others are insulted?

Likewise, if I'm patient   63
   when criticism is directed at others,
seeing it as the arising of mental afflictions,
shouldn't I also remain patient
   when I'm criticized?

With those who destroy stupas or temples,   64   *patience with*
   or harm my teachers, relatives, or friends,   *those who*
I should curb my anger by remembering   65   *harm*
   that such things arise from conditions.

Suffering comes from both animate 66
   and inanimate things,
so why be impatient with only the former?
I should simply endure all harm.

One does harm, the other retaliates with anger; 67
so who's at fault?

The harm I receive is the ripening 68
   of my own karma,
so why should I get angry at others?

Therefore, come what may, 69
I must keep a loving attitude.

Like wisely moving straw away 70
   from a burning house,
I should rid my mind of attachment, 71
   fuel for the anger
   that destroys my precious merit.
For it's far better to give up a few things 72
   and suffer mere human pain
than to suffer in hell.

If this life's problems are unbearable to me, 73
then why don't I abandon the anger
   that will cause much worse?

Many times, on account of my anger,   74
I experienced hellish states
    with no benefit to myself or others.
Now, for the sake of enlightenment,   75
I should joyfully bear a mere fraction of that pain.

Some take great pleasure in praising others;   76   *overcoming*
O mind, why aren't you like that?   *jealousy*
It's a delight encouraged by the sages,   77
    the best way to befriend others.
And if you don't like praising others,   78
then forget rewards in this life and the next!

I wish others to be happy   79
    when I'm being praised,
but when they're praised,
    my joy is so slow in coming.

Having cultivated the mind of enlightenment,   80
how can I be unhappy
    when someone finds happiness?
How can I be jealous when they're praised?   81
Were dependent relatives to find   82
    their own means of livelihood,
would I be annoyed?

How can I have bodhichitta if I'm jealous?   83
Bodhichitta wants happiness for everyone!

Why should I care if someone receives a gift or not?   84
In neither case will it be mine.

This jealousy hinders my good qualities   85
    and lessens people's faith in me.
Shouldn't I resent myself
    for not creating the causes for success?

Not only am I not displeased   86
    at my own misdeeds,
I am jealous of those who do good!

Even if others' misfortune benefits me,   87
how can I possibly take pleasure in it?   88
This deluded state of mind   89
    will certainly cause my downfall.

Praise and reputation don't bring   90   *praise and*
    good health, long life, or merit,   *blame*
    which are all that matter to the wise.   91
Transient pleasures are not true happiness.
Yet for the sake of fame,   92
some sacrifice their wealth.
Why? Can words be eaten?
Will fame please me at death?

When my reputation suffers, I'm like a child   93
    crying before a collapsed sandcastle.

Praise is but a sound; it has no intent to praise me.   94
"My joy comes from others' delight in praising me."
But why should it matter   95
   that praise comes to me or someone else?
For the pleasure belongs to the one who praises.
I should feel delight no matter who's being praised.   96
To feel happy only when I am praised   97
   is childish behavior.

Praise destroys my peace of mind and renunciation   98
and fuels envy of those wiser.
So aren't those who destroy my reputation   99
actually protecting me from wrongdoing?
For fame and possessions are chains   100
   that hinder my wish for liberation,
and those who want to harm me are like buddhas   101
   blocking my rush toward suffering!

Patience is the supreme virtue,   102   *enemies are our*
   and other beings are the cause of it.   *best teachers*
It's my fault if I'm not patient,   103
   obstructing my own practice!
How can the one who's the cause of my patience   104
   be called an obstacle?

A beggar isn't an obstacle to generosity.   105
Beggars are many, offenders few;   106
   for if I don't offend,
   it is likely no one will do me wrong.

Thus enemies are treasures 107
    precious to my spiritual development.
The fruit of my patience arises from our meeting, 108
so let me offer the fruit to them first,
    for they were its cause.

"Honor my enemy? 109
    But he doesn't intend me to perfect patience!"
Well, neither does the Dharma,
    so why honor it?

"He wants to harm me! I can't like him!" 110
But without enemies,
    with whom would I practice patience?
Their harmful intention is the very cause of my patience, 111
and so I must honor my enemies.

Thus beings are merit fields like buddhas; 112   *honoring beings*
by honoring both, many have gone to bliss.   *as much as*
It is by the kindness of both 113   *buddhas*
    that I will become a buddha,
so why honor one but not the other?

It is not their intention that matters 114
    but the effect they have,
and in that they are equal.

Faith in buddhas   115
   and loving intentions toward beings
   both produce much merit.
They are equal in enabling me to become a buddha.   116

Of course ordinary beings don't have   117
   a buddha's infinite qualities.
But the fact that they have buddha potential   118
   makes them a proper object of veneration.

What better way to repay the buddhas' kindness   119   *honoring*
   than to please others?   *others to please*
                                                          buddhas

The buddhas sacrificed their lives for others;   120
I should do no less,
   even for my worst enemy.
How foolish is all this pride of mine!   121
Shouldn't I be humbly serving others instead?

Buddhas are happy when beings are happy   122
   and distressed when they suffer.
So there's no way to delight a buddha   123
   while causing another's pain.

Since the harm I've inflicted on others   124
   saddens the buddhas,

I humbly regret it now
    and pray that they'll bear with me.
From now on, may I master myself   125
    and serve the world
no matter what others do to me,
thus delighting the buddhas!

The compassionate buddhas think of all beings   126
    as themselves,
so how could I despise living beings?

Only by respecting others will I please the buddhas,   127
    accomplish my own aims,
    and eliminate the suffering of the world.
Let this be my vow.

I'll respect my enemies,   128   *conclusion*
    even if they appear weak,   129
for they are protected by both the buddhas   130
    and the guardians of hell.   131
Thus, pleasing beings is the key to enlightenment.   132

Leaving enlightenment aside,   133
    even while still in samsara,   134
patience brings good reputation,
    beauty, health,
    long life, and peace.

7
Joyous Perseverance

With patience, I should cultivate perseverance,   1
for without it enlightenment is impossible.

Joyous perseverance is finding joy in good;   2
laziness, entertainment, and discouragement
   are its obstacles.

ABANDONING OBSTACLES

The source and fuel of *laziness*   3   *laziness*
   are attachment to pleasure
   and disregard for samsara's sufferings.

By the power of my delusions,   4
I'm caught in the cycle of rebirth.
Why don't I realize I am going to die?

Oblivious to my companions dying   5
   one by one,
I'm like a buffalo sleeping soundly
   beside its butcher.

Cornered by death with no escape,   6
how can I take pleasure in food, love, or sleep?

Before it's too late, I should strive   7
   to accumulate merit and wisdom.
For death will appear unexpectedly   8
   amid my half-finished projects.   9
Tormented by the memories of my mistakes,   10
what will I do then?

Thinking of the unbearable agony to come,   11
how can I lie back, carefree?   12
Drawing closer to death with each passing breath,
what a fool I am to think I'm immortal   13
and to dream of the fruit without effort.

With this raft of human birth   14
I should cross the river of pain—
this is no time for sleep!

How can I reject the exquisite joy of Dharma   15   *entertainment*
for *entertainment* that only results in suffering?

Without giving in to *discouragement*,   16   *discouragement*
I should master myself,
then equalize and exchange self for others.

Why be discouraged   17
    when the Buddha explained that with effort   18
    even insects can reach enlightenment?
Shouldn't I, a human discerning right from wrong,   19
    be able to reach enlightenment?

If it's for fear of having to give up this body,   20
then I'm confused about what's hard
    and what's easy.
What is terrible is to suffer eons   21
    without awakening,
whereas hardship on the path to enlightenment   22
    is limited.
Even doctors cause a little suffering   23
    to remove greater pain.
By comparison, the buddhas give gentle treatments   24
    to cure boundless suffering.
Training is gradual: 25
    first give a little food, until eventually   26
    you'll be able to give your body away.

With virtue there would be no pain,   27
with wisdom, no mental afflictions.
Those who take rebirth out of compassion—   28
what could make them suffer?

For through the power of bodhichitta,   29
past negativities are destroyed
   and infinite merit created.
With bodhichitta I'd go from happiness   30
   to happiness,
so how could I be discouraged?

The four powers

To work for the benefit of all, I should cultivate   31
   the supports to my perseverance: 32
the powers of aspiration, self-confidence, joy, and rest.

I *aspire* to destroy the countless delusions of all beings,   33   *aspiration*
even though each one may take eons to conquer.
Though I don't have even a tiny bit of energy to do this,   34
suffering awaits—so I must wake up!

The time has come to develop many good qualities,   35
no matter how long it takes.
So far I've failed to develop any of them,   36
and thus, for nothing have I gained this precious life.

I haven't made offerings   37
   to the buddhas, the Dharma, or the poor;
nor have I offered protection or happiness to anyone.   38
So far my only accomplishment
   has been my mother's labor pains.

In past lives I didn't aspire to the Dharma,   39
which is why I'm in this pitiful state now.
Buddha said that aspiration is the root of all virtues   40
and comes from constant awareness of karma.

Nonvirtuous states of mind   41
   cause physical and mental pain,
while virtuous ones bring happiness.   42
So, however much I strive for happiness,   43
if I do wrong, only suffering will result.
Through virtue I'll be born close to the buddhas,   44
but if I behave unethically,   45
   only the suffering of lower rebirth awaits.

And so I'll develop *aspiration* for virtuous actions   46
and on this basis develop *self-confidence*.

But first let me inspect the task,   47   *self-confidence*
for it's better not to begin
   than to give up once started.
Otherwise this habit will strengthen;   48
I'll achieve nothing and waste my time.

Self-confidence should be applied to three things: 49
   actions, the afflictions, and abilities.

When others, so deluded, are unable to find happiness, 50
I'll be there to help them!
May I do the lowest jobs 51
   without a trace of pride.

If I'm weak, 52
   even the slightest setback will impair me.
The discouraged are easily defeated, 53
so with confidence and perseverance I'll succeed.

The wish to save the world is ridiculous 54
   if I succumb to discouragement.
"Vanquish all and be defeated by nothing"— 55
this is the wholesome pride I should have!

But self-important, destructive pride is the enemy. 56
It prevents all joy 57
   and leads to unfortunate rebirth. 58
Wholesome pride comes from 59
   vanquishing destructive pride.

When overwhelmed by the afflictions, 60
fight them in a thousand ways;
do not surrender!
Despite hardships, bodhisattvas never fall 61
   under the power of the afflictions;
so come what may, 62
I'll never bow to my mental afflictions!

As if playing, whatever action I do,   63   *joy*
    I'll do with *joy*.
People work hard to gain happiness   64
    though success isn't certain;
but those whose joy is in the work itself
will find happiness from their efforts.

Insatiably chasing sensory pleasure,   65
    like honey on a razor's edge,
why not instead chase merit
    that leads to endless goodness?

With joyful perseverence,   66
I should commit to this work
and bring it to completion.

If tired, I should *rest* for a while.   67   *rest*

Like a warrior, I'll always be on guard   68   *commitment*
    against delusions
    and vigorously counter-attack them.
And if I drop the sword of mindfulness,   69
I will quickly pick it up.

Just as poison spreads in the blood,   70
faults spread in my mind if I allow them.

So I'll be vigilant of disturbing thoughts,   71
like a frightened man threatened with death
    if he lets a single drop spill from a full jar.
Alert as if a snake were nearby,   72
I'll watch for sleep and laziness.

Each mistake I'll confess and think,   73
    "What can I do so this never happens again?"
I'll seek the company of the wise   74
    to develop mindfulness in every situation.
Before doing any action,   75
    I'll recall this advice on mindfulness
    and joyfully rise to the challenge.

As a flower seed carried by the wind,   76
may I be lifted by joyful perseverance
    and thus attain my goals.

8
Meditative Concentration

A distracted mind will naturally dwell
    between the fangs of delusions.
Therefore cultivate meditative concentration.

      1

Physical and mental isolation
    reduce the chances of mental wandering,
so let go of this worldly life.

      2   *attachment to worldly life*

Craving for love and gain
    prevents me from renouncing worldly concerns.

      3

Insight and stability stop disturbing thoughts.
Understanding this, I must first develop stability,
achieved by abandoning attachment.

      4

If I, one transient being, am obsessed with another,
for lifetimes we won't meet again;

      5   *attachment to people*

I'll be unable to meditate without seeing him or her
    and be tortured by desire even if I do.

      6

Longing for the beloved prevents the detachment   7
   required to see reality.
Obsessed by family and friends   8
I'll fail to reach freedom,
and this precious life will have been in vain.

Imitating the childish will lead me to hell;   9
why stay with them?
One moment friends, the next enemies;   10
it is so hard to satisfy the childish!
Wise words irritate them   11
while they turn me away from what is beneficial
and get upset if I don't listen to them.
Envious of superiors,   12
   competitive with equals,
   arrogant toward inferiors,
   and easily enraged:
what good was ever had from these folks?

Praising oneself,   13
   belittling others,
   gossiping about worldly pleasures—
associating with such people only brings problems.   14
I will live in solitude, the mind at peace.

When meeting childish beings,   15
I'll conduct myself kindly
   without becoming overly familiar.

Thus taking only what benefits the mind,   16
I won't get attached to anyone.

I'll be wary of seeking fame and wealth,   17   *attachment to*
for death will come suddenly.   *wealth and*
                                                                      fame

No matter what I'm attached to,   18
I'll crave for more
   and suffer endlessly.
From attachment arises fear.   19
So like the wise, understand that at death
   all craved objects fade to nothing.
The rich and famous have been plentiful,   20
   yet who remembers them now?

One day I'll be praised   21
   and another despised.
So why be happy or unhappy about it?
If even the Buddha couldn't please everyone,   22
   how can I?
So why worry whether people like me?
They despise the poor, criticize the rich—   23
I could never please them anyway!
The narrow-minded like no one   24
   except out of self-interest.
Love tainted with self-interest
   is nothing other than self-love.

In the forest, the trees, birds, and deer   25   *benefits of*
   never say anything unpleasant.   *solitude*
Oh, when will I live among them?
When will I go, never looking back,   26
to dwell in empty temples,
   at the foot of trees,
   or in caves?
When will I live in such retreat places,   27
   unclaimed and ownerless,
   remaining free and detached?
When might I live without fear,   28
having just a bowl
   and a few old clothes?

When, having gone to the cemetery,   29
will I see the similarity between my body
   and the corpses there?
My body will become a putrid thing,   30
   its stench repellant even to animals.

My bones will be dispersed,   31
as will all my friends.
Alone we are born, alone we die.   32
As nobody can take away our pain,
   what are friends if not obstacles?
We pass through this life like travelers   33
   stopping for the night.

So before death comes,   34
let me go into solitude,
where, without intimate friends or conflicts,   35
    already dead to the world,
    there'll be no mourners at my passing
and no one to distract me   36
    from being mindful of Buddha.

Thus, in lovely places with little trouble,   37
let me dwell in solitude, quieting all distractions.
There, focusing on one intent,   38
I'll strive to settle and tame my mind
    in absorbed concentration.

Desire is a source of pain in this life   39   *disenchantment*
    and the next.   *with desire*

For the sake of an embrace,   40
I've created so much negative karma.   41
And yet that body I ardently desired   42
was in truth nothing but a corpse.

That face I liked so much   43
    and was so protective of—
why don't I like it now that   44
    vultures have done their work?   45
It's this future corpse I now adorn with gifts.   46
I shiver at the thought of a motionless corpse;   47
why not now while it's moving?

I don't lust after a naked corpse; 48
why now while it's adorned and covered?

Both saliva and excrement come from food, 49
so why like one and shun the other?
Pillows are soft to touch; 50
shouldn't I like to fondle them too? 51

Is it my obsession with my own body's impurities 52
that makes me long for another bag of filth? 53

"But it's the flesh I enjoy." 54
How can I desire something that is mindless?
My beloved's mind can't be seen or touched, 55
and their tangible body is without consciousness.

I may ignore that another's body 56
   is full of impurities,
but how can I forget the impure nature of my own?
Why delight in a container of filth 57
and ignore a fresh lotus blossom
   opened in the sunlight of a cloudless sky?

I wouldn't touch excrement, 58
yet I long for a body born from impurities and full of it. 59
I have no wish for worms born in filth; 60
well, wasn't this body born in it too?
Not only am I not disgusted at my own uncleanness, 61
   but I desire another impure body too!

Even tasty food, when expelled from the mouth,   62
   makes the floor dirty.

If I still don't believe in my body's impurity,   63
I should gaze upon fetid corpses.
Having seen their skin removed,   64
how could I take pleasure in a body again?

The smell I love comes from perfume;   65
why get attached to a body with a foreign smell?
If I'm repulsed by the body's natural foul smell,   66
   isn't that good?
How is it that the smell of perfume   67
   makes me long for something else?

If left untended the body, unwashed,   68
   with long hair and nails and yellow teeth,
   is repelling.
So why pamper what is but a weapon   69
   for inflicting self-harm?
This world is full of fools!
If I'm disgusted by skeletons in cemeteries,   70
why not by walking corpses-to-be?

That desired, impure body   71   *price of*
   is not gained without effort;   *satisfying desire*
for its sake you have to work hard!
Young, you work so hard to keep a spouse,   72
then later you're too old to satisfy your lust!

Some work the whole day for money   73
and in the evening lie exhausted like a corpse.
Others travel abroad looking for work,   74
separated from the family they're working for!
Some sell themselves   75
    out of confused self-interest
and toil pointlessly
    at the whim of others.
Others must travel continuously,   76
leaving their family behind
    to fend for themselves.

Blinded by desire, foolish people look for fortune   77   *futility of*
    but find only slavery.   *seeking wealth*
Much suffering is endured   78
    in the search for wealth.
The pain related to earning,   79
    conserving,
    or losing wealth
    renders it a great misfortune.
So much misery for such a tiny bit of happiness!   80
It's a tough trade   81
    to waste this precious human life
    for little pleasures even an animal can get.

Since beginningless time,   82
    we've gone through so much pain
    for transient pleasures.
Yet with a thousand times less effort,   83
we could have reached enlightenment itself.

Desire produces the sufferings of hell;   84
what could be worse than that?

By this contemplation   85   *joy in solitude*
may I become disillusioned with desires
and find the peace and joy of solitude!
Fortunate are those who roam in nature,   86
reflecting on their aims of benefiting others,
free of cares,   87
    dwelling in solitary places as long as they please.
Without attachment to anyone or anything,   88
they taste a happiness even devas don't enjoy.

Having thus considered the excellence of solitude,   89
I will fully quiet my rambling thoughts
and meditate on bodhichitta.

EQUALITY OF SELF AND OTHERS

First I'll reflect on the equality of myself and others,   90   *conventional*
as we're all alike in joy and sorrow.   *equality*

As I care for my body with its many limbs 91
    as a whole,
so should I care for all beings,
    one in wanting to be happy.

Pain that's mine is hard to bear 92
    because of clinging to "me."
Likewise, the pain of another isn't felt by "me" 93
but by the other from clinging to their "me."
Therefore I should alleviate others' pain, 94
    for it's simply pain, like my own;
and I'll benefit others,
    living beings just like me.

We all equally want happiness; 95
why only care for mine? 96

"Their pains don't affect me." 97
Then why worry about my future pain,
    which doesn't harm my present "me"?

"Because it will be me!" 98
Wrong. The present-moment I perishes
    and another I will be born.

"It's for the sufferer to protect himself."   99
Why then does the hand
   protect the suffering of the foot?

"It might be illogical, but it's because of feeling   100
   the whole body-mind to be 'me.'"
Well, shouldn't we reject what's illogical?

Aggregates, armies, forests   101   *ultimate*
   are not truly findable wholes;   *equality*
so since no possessor of suffering exists,
   to whom does it belong?
And if all pains are without an owner,   102
I should dispel them all, without distinction,
   simply because they hurt.

"If there are no suffering beings,   103
   what suffering is there to alleviate?"
In that case, alleviate either everyone's or no one's
   but not just your own.

"With compassion much suffering arises,   104   *universal*
   so why develop it?"   *compassion*
Well, compared to the suffering of the world,
   it's not very much.

If the suffering of many can be stopped 105
   by that of one,
someone with loving compassion
   would seek to bring it on.
That's why some bodhisattvas sacrifice their lives 106
   to save the lives of many.
Wishing to alleviate the suffering of others, 107
they happily enter the deepest hells.

Saving others, they receive oceans of joy; 108
why settle for pale liberation?
Helping others and their happiness 109
   is itself my satisfaction—
   without pride, conceit, or expectations.

Just as I protect myself 110
   from even the smallest problem,
with compassion I'll do the same for others.
Through habit I attach the notion of "me" 111
   to the sperm and ovum of others;
so why not consider the body of another as "me"? 112

EXCHANGING MYSELF WITH OTHERS

Reflect on the faults of self-cherishing 113
   and the benefits of cherishing others
and then train in the exchange.

Just as I see my limbs as part of a bigger whole—　　　114
　　my body—
why not see embodied beings
　　as part of a whole humanity?

If through habit I regard this body,　　　115
　　devoid of a self, as "me,"
likewise through habit I could regard others as "me."

So if others are me, I shouldn't expect any reward　　　116
　　from helping them,
　　as I wouldn't for helping myself.
And just as I protect "myself" from misery,　　　117
protecting "others" can become second nature.
Avalokiteshvara blessed even his name,　　　118
so that by recollecting it
　　beings could overcome fear.
Don't think it impossible, for　　　119
　　through familiarity
we can even learn to love
　　those we once feared.

Whoever wishes to quickly free himself and others　　　120
should train in this most sacred secret:
　　the exchange of self with others.

The self-cherishing mind hates sickness and hunger 121
   and longs for honor and comfort.
It will go as far as killing animals, 122
   even father or mother, 123
   to reach its aim.
So see this selfish attachment to the body 124
   as an enemy, only creating negative karma.

Go from 125 *comparing*
   "If I give this away, what will remain for me?" *selfishness and*
to *altruism*
   "If I keep this, what will be left to give?"

Using others for myself brings suffering; 126
using myself for others, bliss.

Wanting the best for me 127
   brings low status and rebirth.
Shifting this wish to others
   brings honor and good rebirths.

Making others work for me 128
   brings rebirth as a servant,
working for others,
   rebirth as a lord.

All joy comes from wishing others happiness,   129
all misery from self-cherishing.
Just look at the difference   130
   between lowly beings who work for themselves
   and sages who work for the good of others!

Without exchanging self for others,   131
enlightenment will not be gained,
   nor even happiness in this world.
In this life, all hell will break loose;   132
   servants won't work, masters won't pay.
Instead of working for one another,   133
   the source of happiness,
ignorant people harm one another
   and pay a high price in unbearable suffering.

If all the pain in the world   134
   comes from grasping at an "I,"
why even tolerate this enemy?
As long as I don't abandon it, I'll suffer,   135
just as a fire will continue to burn me
   until I drop it from my hands.

So to free myself and others from suffering,   136
I'll give myself to others
   and cherish them as I do myself.

O mind, you now belong to others.   137
Other than their welfare,
 you won't think of anything else.
My body will only move for the benefit of others; 138
anything I own will only be used for them.   139

In order to generate compassion,   140 *exchanging*
let me trade places   *with thoughts*
by identifying myself as "others"
and viewing "me"
 with envy, competitiveness, and pride:

"What? He's so well treated and honored. 141 *envy of a*
But look at me—   *subordinate*
 I'm despised and don't earn as much."
"I work while he rests.   142
People think he's great and I'm inferior,
 without qualities."
"Without qualities? Not true!   143
He's lower than some,
 while I'm superior to some."
"It's because of delusions   144
 that my practice and morality have declined.
Being helpless, I wish he'd heal me."
"But he does nothing and despises me. 145
What use are his qualities to me?
He has no compassion for me,   146
yet pretends to be so wise."

"He who's considered my equal,   147   *rivalry of a*
I'll beat in wealth and honor,   *peer*
   regardless of the consequences.
May my qualities be known to all and his ignored.   148
May my failings remain hidden   149
   and all honor be kept for me,
while I delight at his public demise."   150

"Look at this miserable one   151   *pride of a*
   who dares compete with me   *superior*
   in learning, intelligence, and wealth!
Hearing my praises   152
   sends shivers of joy down my spine.
I will take what he owns by force   153
and leave him just enough to serve me.
Knowing that I suffered over and over   154
   in samsara because of him,
from now on he'll have no happiness."

O mind, for so many lives   155   *ending the*
   you looked after your self-interest in this way   *bondage of*
and only experienced pain.   *selfishness*
I must trust and follow Buddha's advice   156
and later experience its advantages.
Had I had done so earlier,   157
I wouldn't be in this pitiful state now.

Just as I placed the notion of "me" 158
   onto the sperm and ovum of my parents,
I'll do the same onto the bodies of others.

Having exchanged myself for others, 159 *exchanging*
I'll use whatever I possess for others' benefit. *with actions*
And shouldn't I be envious of that "me" 160
   that is happy while others are sad,
   that merely seeks its own interest?

I'll leave my happiness behind 161
   and embrace the pain of others;
Take the blame for others' faults 162
   and openly admit even my minor faults.
By praising others, 163
   I'll make their fame outshine my own,
   and always serve them,
hiding any qualities I might have, 164
   so no one knows them.

In brief, may all the harm I've done to others 165
   come back to me.
May I be free of arrogance 166
   and act as shy as a young bride.

From now on I'll be tough on you, O mind,　　　167
and you will abandon your selfish ways.
You, the cause of all my suffering,　　　168
　　wherever you go,
　　I'll destroy your arrogance.　　　169
I've offered you to others, so be of service!　　　170

If I don't give you to others,　　　171
without a doubt you'll lead me to hell.
How many times have you brought me there?　　　172
Remembering your selfishness, I'll subdue you.

If I want happiness,　　　173
　　I should cherish others.
If I want protection,
　　I should protect others.

The more I pamper this body,　　　174　　*giving up this*
the more temperamental it becomes;　　　　　　*body for others*
and the more temperamental,　　　175
the more I crave to satisfy it,
　　but to no avail.
This craving is misery;　　　176
those who are free from it
　　find everlasting peace.
So I won't let physical desires increase　　　177
and will surround myself with things
　　that don't arouse desire.

Why get attached to this impure body,   178
   which will end up as ashes?
What use is this machine to me, alive or dead?   179
Oh, feeling of "I," why won't you die?
Attachment to my body has only brought me pain;   180
why care about its loves or hates?
This body doesn't care about its own fate,   181
   so why should I protect it?
Nor does it know anger or pleasure,   182
   so why exhaust myself on its behalf?

"I like my body—it and I are friends."   183
Well, since all beings like their bodies,
why don't I find pleasure in theirs?
I'll give up this body for the sake of others   184
and look after it like I would a tool.

Enough of my childish ways!   185   *resolve*
I'll follow the wise and avoid sleep and laziness.
If I don't make constant effort, day and night,   186
when will my suffering come to an end?
To eliminate delusions, I'll constantly rest my mind   187
   with meditative concentration
   on the perfect object, emptiness.

9
Wisdom

All that precedes, Buddha taught as a preparation   1
    for us to understand
    how things really exist.
Those wishing to bring an end to suffering
    should strive to realize it.

Things exist on two levels simultaneously: 2   *Madhyamika's*
the ultimate level,   *presentation of*
    which can't be perceived by an ordinary conceptual mind,   *the two truths*
and the conventional one,
    which can.

In this context, people are seen to be of two kinds: 3
    the ordinary person and the yogi.
The views of the former are undermined by that of the
    latter.

Yogis themselves vary in their degrees of insight.   4
In their debates, they use commonly accepted analogies—
    such as a magician's illusion—
to demonstrate that
    although something may appear to the mind,
it isn't necessarily real.

Although things appear alike   5
    to yogis and ordinary people,
the latter believe them to be self-existent
    and not illusion-like.
It is in this regard that they disagree.

Since form and so forth   6   *general*
    are established by direct perception,   *refutation of*
isn't it contradictory to say that they are false?   *self-existence*

No, because objects of direct perception such as form
    appear to be self-existent,
but this is not a valid perception of their ultimate nature,
    just as we mistakenly perceive the unclean body
    to be clean.

In order to guide beings gradually,   7
    the Buddha first taught phenomena to be impermanent.

If ultimately things aren't impermanent,
isn't it a contradiction
    to say that they are so conventionally?

There is no contradiction. 8
For on a conventional level, compared to
   the ordinary person's view of things as permanent,
the yogi's view of them as impermanent is correct—
   as is his apprehension of the body as unclean.

If all phenomena were unreal, 9
   then the Buddha also would be unreal.
So how could we accumulate merit from honoring him?

In the same way that you believe self-existent merits
   are accumulated from honoring a self-existent Buddha,
likewise for us, illusory merits can be obtained
   from honoring an illusory Buddha.

But if beings were unreal, 10
   how could you explain rebirth?

For as long as the necessary conditions are assembled,
   for that long illusion will occur.
Why merely by their longer duration should beings be
   more real than illusions?

If beings were illusions, 11
   they would have no mind.
Then how could killing an illusory being be evil?

Beings do possess illusion-like minds;
therefore evils and merits do arise in relation to them.

If the real person 12
    and the one created by the magician
    are similar in being illusions,
how can one have mind and not the other?

The causes of the magician's illusion are spells and other
    tricks that can't give rise to mind.
Beings and illusions have different causes,
and nowhere is there one cause that has the ability
    to produce all effects.

If while being ultimately liberated, 13
    one were still conventionally subject to rebirth,
then even a buddha would be subject to rebirth.
Therefore what use would there be
    to pursue the bodhisattva way of life?

Beings will remain in cyclic existence 14
    as long as ignorance, its cause, has not been removed.
But since a buddha has removed these causes,
    even conventionally
    he is no longer subject to rebirth.

Chittamatrin: If you say that mind 15   *critique of the*
    doesn't ultimately exist   *Chittamatra*
then what is it that perceives?   *view*
And without a perceiver, how can you posit
    any objects of perception?

But for you external objects don't exist,   16
    so what is perceived anyway?

We believe that mind exists
    and external objects don't
and that the objects that appear to mind
    are of the same nature as mind.

If the mind and the object it apprehends   17
    are of the same nature,
    subject and object would be one.
In which case, what object would be perceived
    by what mind?
The Buddha said that mind cannot perceive mind,
    just like a sword can't cut itself.

The mind perceives itself   18
    just like a light illuminates itself.

A light doesn't illuminate itself
because the light has never been dark;
as soon as a light is lit,
    it is not obscured by any darkness.

A blue thing does not require   19
    another blue thing for its blueness,
    as does a clear crystal.

Likewise the mind is seen sometimes to depend
  on an object to arise
  and sometimes not.

Your example is invalid   20
  because there is no blue object that is blue by itself.
Blueness depends on other conditions.

When being perceived by mind,   21
  it can be said that a lamp illuminates itself.
But when being perceived by what mind
  could it be said that mind perceives itself?

Since the mind cannot be subject and object   22
  at the same time,
  nothing observes the mind,
so it is as meaningless to discuss
  self-perceiving moments of awareness
  as it is talking about
  the beauty of a barren woman's daughter.

If the mind cannot perceive itself,   23
  how can you explain that mind remembers?

Memory is induced by the perception of something else,
as when the memory of having been bitten by a rat
  is triggered by the ensuing pain.

We know that in certain conditions 24
  mind can perceive the minds of others.
How then, could it not perceive itself?

That one can see something distant
  does not necessarily imply
  that one can see what is near.
Take the example of a special eye-ointment:
  it may enable one to see a buried pot,
  but the ointment itself on the eye can't be seen.

Without self-perception 25
  there can be no memory.
And without self-perception
  the experience of the object of sight doesn't exist.

We do not seek to refute
  what is seen, heard, or cognized
but rather the belief in the true existence of these
  phenomena, which is the cause of suffering.

External objects are not other than mind, 26
nor are they mind itself.

How could this possibly be?
A thing that is neither the mind nor other than it
  could not exist.

Although objects are not really existent,   27
  they can be seen.

Likewise we say that the mind,
  although not really existent,
  can nevertheless perceive.

Cyclic existence,
  the state in which subject and object
  appear as two substantially distinct things,
has to have something real as the base,
  namely truly existent, nondual consciousness.
Otherwise cyclic existence would be similar to space.

If, as you say, the dualistic state of cyclic existence   28
  relied upon a self-existent basis,
how could it have the function of appearing
  as real subject and object?
In your tradition, whatever is mind would become
  a solitary nondual consciousness
  unassisted by any object.

And if the mind were freed   29
  from the dualistic appearances of subject-object,
all beings would already be buddhas,
so what benefit is gained in speculating
  that the mind and its object are mind only?

Realist: How does knowing things to be illusion-like   30
  prevent mental distortions from arising?
Doesn't a magician still desire
  the illusory women he creates?

*refuting that
emptiness is not
necessary to
reach liberation*

Yes he does,   31
  because he hasn't yet freed himself
  of the tendency of the mental distortions.
So when he gazes upon the illusory woman,
the habit of seeing her emptiness is weak.

However, by familiarizing the mind with emptiness,   32
  the tendency to perceive things as inherently existent,
  emptiness itself included,
  will gradually fade.
At that time, it will be impossible
  for mental distortions to arise.

When it is said that no thing exists, it means that   33
  when analyzed
  the self-existence of things is not found.
Then how could this non-self-existence,
  which has no foundation,
  be truly existent?

When neither a self-existent thing   34
  nor a self-existent emptiness
  appear to the mind,

all apprehensions of self-existence cease,
and the mind,
   being without such objective support,
   is totally pacified.

If free of conceptual motivation   35
   how can a buddha think
   "I will benefit others"?

Like wish-granting trees and jewels help beings
   without having the concept "I will help,"
so the Buddha benefits beings
   without thinking "I will benefit."
He benefits due to the power of
   his aspiration created when he was a bodhisattva
   and due to the merits of his disciples.

Since the aspiration prayers of bodhisattvas cease   36
   when they become buddhas,
how could they still have effect at that time?

They can, just like a medicinal pillar neutralizes poisons
   even after its maker has passed away.
Similarly, a buddha,   37
   even though free of conceptual desire to help,
nevertheless effortlessly manifests to fulfill beings' needs,
motivated by the aspiration prayers he made
   in his previous lives as a bodhisattva.

How can offerings to Buddha, 38
   who has no conceptual mind,
   bear fruit if he's unable to consciously accept them?

Whether Buddha is alive or has passed away,
it is said that the offerings made to him or to his relics
   have equal merit.
The scriptures state that it doesn't matter 39
   whether one perceives the offerings
   or Buddha as truly existent.
In both cases merit is accumulated.

Vaibashika: Realizing the four noble truths is enough 40
   to reach liberation.
What use then is there for realizing emptiness?

Because the Mahayana scriptures state that without it,
   there is no liberation.

We don't accept 41   *authenticity of*
   the Mahayana scriptures as authentic.   *scriptures*
Only ours are authentic
   because both Hinayanists and Mahayanists accept them.

If being validated authenticates a scripture
then your own scriptures were not authenticated by you
   before you studied and analyzed them.

The criteria you uphold   42
   for authenticating the Hinayana scriptures
   also applies to the Mahayana,
because we too have an unbroken lineage of teachers.
And if you believe something to be true merely because
   two people accept it,
then the Vedas and other non-Buddhist scriptures
   would also be true.

Mahayana is to be rejected   43
   since its authenticity is contested.

Then you might as well abandon your own scriptures,
for their validity too is contested
   by non-Buddhists and even some Buddhists.

Most of the Mahayana sutras   44
   are similar to the Hinayana sutras;
therefore why not acknowledge them as Buddha's words?

If the entire Mahayana is deemed corrupt   45
   due to one exception,
why not equally claim that all are authentic
   on the basis of one Mahayana sutra
   being comparable to the Hinayana?

If even the great Kashyapa and others   46
   found these teachings hard to understand,

who would consider them as invalid
    simply because you don't understand them?

You might insist that the root for establishing   47
    the presence of the Buddha's teaching
    is the sangha of arhats.
But it is unlikely that those ordained were arhats,
    for those whose minds grasp at true existence
    cannot achieve nirvana.

For becoming an arhat,   48
it is not necessary to realize emptiness.
Through familiarity with the sixteen aspects of the four truths,
one abandons delusions and reaches liberation.

No, what you describe only temporarily liberates
    from manifest delusions.
Therefore such a person hasn't reached nirvana
and has still the karmic potential
    to take rebirth in cyclic existence.

Because those arhats   49
    have completely abandoned
    attachment to the aggregates,
    the principal cause of rebirth in samsara,
they have abandoned delusions forever
and therefore will not take rebirth.

According to the Abhidharma
   there are two types of attachments:
   deluded and nondeluded.
The arhats as you describe them are still subject
   to the nondeluded attachments.

Craving arises from sensation,   50
   and they still have sensation.
As long as they still hold those sensations
   to be truly existent,
attachment to things will arise.

Just as delusions are temporally stopped   51
   in a state of deep concentration,
so it is for those "arhats" who haven't realized emptiness.
Therefore one should strive to realize it.

In order to work for the welfare of others,   52
bodhisattvas abide in samsara,
   free of fear and attachment.
Such are the fruits
   that the realization of emptiness bears.

Since no refutation of emptiness can hold its ground,   53
let us cultivate its realization.

Emptiness is the antidote to disturbing emotions 54
 and the obscuration to knowledge.
Therefore, how could those who wish to attain omniscience not cultivate it?

Why be afraid of emptiness, 55
 which pacifies all suffering?
Rather we should fear the apprehension of true existence,
 since it's the source of suffering.

MEDITATION ON THE SELFLESSNESS
OF PERSON

If there were such a thing as an I, 56
 indeed fear could arise.
But since no I exists at all,
 who has fear?

No parts of the body, 57
 such as the teeth, hair, nails, bones, or blood,
 are the I.
Neither inner organs nor grease, sweat, or waste 58
 are the I.
The flesh, skin, body's warmth, and breath 59
 are not the I.
Nor is it found in the body's cavities
or within any one of the six consciousnesses.

How can a self or consciousness   60
   that enjoys the five sense objects
    be unchanging?
If, for example, the consciousness that apprehends sound
   were unchanging,
it would always apprehend sound.
But in the absence of sound,
how can a consciousness of sound be posited?

refutation of the self postulated by the Samkhyas

If consciousness, whose function is to cognize,   61
   could exist in the absence
   of an object of cognition,
    then even a piece of wood would be conscious.

Therefore without an object,
consciousness cannot exist.

Samkhya: When there is no sound,   62
consciousness apprehends something else,
   such as visual form.

At that moment, why doesn't consciousness
   apprehend sound?

Because sound is no longer there.

Neither then is consciousness of sound.

And how can something whose nature it is 63
    to apprehend sound
ever apprehend visual form?

You maintain it's possible in the same way as
    a given man can be both father and son.
But father and son are a mere designation
    and don't exist intrinsically.

The primal substance cannot be at the same time 64
    father and son
because for you this primal substance
    has true independent existence.
Moreover we have never observed
    a consciousness of form perceiving sound.

It is like an actor changing roles. 65

Then it is not unchanging.

It is of the same permanent underlying nature;
only its aspect changes.

Something of a permanent nature
    that is identical with something that changes
has never been seen before.

Consciousness appears superficially   66
   in various ways
but has one permanent true underlying nature,
that of being merely conscious.

That would imply that all beings are one,
since all beings' different streams of consciousnesses
have an underlying nature of being just consciousness.

If multiple entities are one due to a single similarity,   67
then consciousness and primordial substance
   would be one as well,
for they are alike in being existent.

And if, as you say,
   the manifestations of primordial substance are false,
how could what it manifests from be real?

Matter cannot be the self   68   *refutation of the*
since it is not conscious,   *self postulated*
   just like a vase.   *by Naiyayikas*
                                        and Vaisheshikas

Naiyayika: Although not conscious
it is conjoined with consciousness
   and thus aware.

In that case, the previously unconscious self
would change by becoming conscious
and therefore could not be unchangeable.

If, as you say, the self is unchangeable,   69
how could consciousness affect it?

And if you accept the self as lacking in consciousness
    because it is matter,
and separated from the function of producing effects
    because it is permanent,
then space could also be a self.

Non-Buddhist: Without a permanent self,   70   *refutation of*
there would be no link between actions   *a permanent,*
    and their results.   *partless, and*
If the subject perished after having acted,   *independent self*
who would experience the karmic result?

The aggregates of this life   71
    that create the action
and the aggregates of the future life
    that experience its effect
are distinct.

Since you posit an unchanging self
that can neither commit an action
    nor experience its effect
and we don't posit a self that commits an action
    or experiences its effect,
is it not meaningless to argue this point?

It is not possible to see at the same time   72
the one that creates the action
and the one that experiences its result,
just as a father and a son cannot be born at the same time.

The self or I that creates
and the self that experiences its result
are simply imputed
    on the continuum of the same aggregates.

But why is there not a permanent self?   73

The past or the future moments of consciousness
are not the I
for they are not existent now.

Isn't the mind of the present moment,
    which has been produced but has not yet ceased,
the self?

If that were the case, then in the next moment,
    when it had perished,
it would no longer be the self.
With the same reasoning all five aggregates
can be rejected as being the self.

Just as when the bark of a banana tree is taken away,   74
    nothing is found inside,
likewise when the truly existent self is sought,
    it is not found among the aggregates.

If no beings truly exist,   75
for whom is compassion generated?

One develops compassion for those
    designated as beings by the confused mind
in order to lead them to the goal of liberation.

If beings do not truly exist,   76
who gains the fruit of enlightenment?

True, ultimately nobody.
But conventionally we accept a person
    whose virtuous actions lead to enlightenment.

Since compassion arises from a mind confused   77
    about how things exist,
surely compassion is fit to be rejected,
as is confusion about the self.

One shouldn't reject compassion;
it helps to completely pacify suffering.
But confusion about the self should be rejected,

because it increases such things as self-importance
    that are causes for suffering.
For this, meditation upon selflessness
    is the supreme remedy.

The selflessness of phenomena

The body is not the feet, calves, thighs, hips,   78   *selflessness*
    abdomen, back, chest, or arms.   *of the body*
It is not the hands, torso, armpits,   79
    shoulders, neck, or head.
Then where is this truly existent body?

If the body as a whole is distinct from its individual parts   80
    yet pervades all of them,
this suggests that the body itself is not composed of parts.
How then does it exist?

If the truly existent body were located in its entirety   81
    in the hand and other limbs,
there would be just as many bodies
    as there are hands and so forth.

If the truly existent body is found neither inside   82
    nor on the surface of its parts,
how can it reside in its parts?
And as it is not found separately from its parts,
how can it exist at all?

Thus, while the body does not truly exist,   83
because of a misperception a body appears to the mind
    on the basis of its parts.
Just like the mind mistakes a pile of stones for a person
    because of having a similar shape.
As long as the conditions are assembled,   84
the pile of stones will appear as a person
and the limbs and so forth as a body.

In the same way, since the hand is only   85
    an assembly of parts such as fingers,
how can the hand truly exist?
The same reasoning can be applied to fingers and joints.

These parts too break down into atoms,   86
which break down further into directional particles
    and so on
until nothing remains.
Thus atoms are empty as space,
    devoid of true existence.

Then what discerning person would be attached   87
    to this form that is just like a dream?
Since the body does not truly exist,
how can the distinction be made
between truly existent male and female bodies?

If pain existed truly, it would never cease. 88
Why then does it not prevent joyful experiences
    from arising?
Likewise, if pleasure existed truly,
why don't pleasant tastes comfort a man in grief?

You may say pain is not experienced 89
    because it's overpowered by pleasure.
But then how can that which is not experienced
    be a feeling of pain?

You may say that the subtle pain that remains 90
is less intense than the previous pain,
so it becomes like subtle pleasure.
Then that subtle pleasure is pleasure, not pain.

If pain is not produced 91
    in the absence of contributing conditions,
does it not imply that pain is merely a conceptual
    designation on the collection of contributing conditions?

This analysis is cultivated as an antidote 92
    to these wrong conceptions of self-existence.
Familiarization with this insight
supported by meditative stabilization
feeds the inner experience of the contemplatives.

If there is a space between a sense organ
   and its object,
how can they ever enter into contact?
And if there is no space between them,
   they would occupy the same space
   and thus would be one.
In which case, what would come into contact with what?

93   *emptiness of a*
truly existent
contact that
causes feeling

One partless particle cannot penetrate another,
because it is without inner space
   and both are the same size.
When there is no penetration, there is no mingling,
and when there is no mingling, there is no contact.

94

How, indeed, can there be contact
   with something that has no parts?
If partlessness can be observed when there is contact,
   demonstrate this.

95

It is impossible for an immaterial
   self-existent consciousness
to have contact with self-existent physical particles.
And it is invalid to say that the mere aggregation
   of the sense faculty, the object, and consciousness
produce the effect of a cognition,
because just as we analyzed before,
an aggregation is not found
   to be a truly existent thing.

96   *absence of*
truly existent
contact between
consciousness
and matter

Thus, if there is no contact,　　　　　　　　　　97
　　how can feeling arise?
Why exert oneself to avoid pain?
Who could be harmed by what?

Understanding that there is no one to experience feeling　　98
and that feelings don't exist,
why not give up this craving for feelings?

That which is seen and that which is touched　　　　99
are of a dream-like nature.
And because feelings arise simultaneously with mind,
they are not ultimately perceived.

Past feelings are only remembered　　　　　　100
future ones are not yet felt.
Feeling doesn't feel itself,
nor is it experienced by something else.

There is no self-existent person who experiences feeling　　101
and no self-existent feeling.
Therefore who can be benefited by pleasure
　　or hurt by pain?

The mind is not in the sense organs,　　　　　102　　*emptiness of a*
not in the sense objects,　　　　　　　　　　　　　　　*truly existent*
nor in between.　　　　　　　　　　　　　　　　　　　*mind*

The mind is neither found inside
   nor outside the body,
nor anywhere else.

This absence of the self-existence of beings' minds   103
   is nirvana.

If awareness existed prior to the object of awareness,   104
   in dependence on what would this awareness arise?
If they arose simultaneously,   105
   likewise in dependence on what would it arise?
And if it arose after its object has ceased,
   from what would this awareness arise?
In this way it is ascertained that
   no phenomenon comes truly into existence.

If nothing existed truly   106
   then conventional truth would not exist,
in which case how could there be two truths?

And if phenomena only existed as mere convention,
   there would be no cause and effect;
then how could there be a path to liberation?

One cannot claim that something is said to exist   107
merely because it is conceived by a deluded mind.

What we mean by conventional truth is
that which is established by a valid mind
   onto a valid basis of imputation.
Therefore things do function.

The designating mind and its designated object   108
   are mutually dependent,
just as any analysis into ultimate reality
   is dependent upon what is commonly known.

Wouldn't it also be necessary   109
   to analyze the analyzing mind
to see whether it has ultimate existence?
But if the analyzing mind were subject to analysis,
one would need to analyze that one, too,
   and so on, ad infinitum.

When an object is analyzed,   110
no basis for analysis remains.
Subject and object will be seen to lack inherent existence,
and that is called *nirvana.*

REFUTING OTHERS' CONCEPTIONS OF TRUE EXISTENCE

If an object exists inherently   111   *refuting truly*
   because the mind inherently exists,   *existent subject*
how does one prove the inherent existence of the mind?   *and object*

And if the inherent existence of the mind is established   112
    on the base of the inherent existence of the object,
then what proof is there
    of the inherent existence of the object?
Since their existences are mutually dependent,
neither can exist inherently.

Just as father and son cannot be posited   113
    in the absence of the other,
likewise mind and its object depend on each other
and hence lack inherent existence.

Realist: On the contrary, dependence proves true existence.   114
One can infer the true existence of a seed
    by the fact that it produces a sprout.
And since awareness arises in dependence on an object,
    why can't it prove its true existence?

This is not the same thing.   115
In the case of a sprout, a consciousness different from it
    can infer the existence of a seed.
But in the case of consciousness,
    while apprehending an object,
by what verifying cognition
    is that awareness of the object ascertained?

DIAMOND SLIVER REASONING

Charvaka: A phenomenon arises without causes
   and exists by its own nature.

116   *refuting production from no causes*

Everybody can see directly
   that inner and outer phenomena have causes.
Various effects, such as the stem of a lotus,
   are produced by a variety of causes.

What makes the various causes?

117

A preceding variety of causes.

What makes a distinct cause
   able to produce a distinct effect?

The power of each effect's preceding causes.

You say Ishvara, who is the collection of
   the four elements of earth, water, fire, and air,
is the cause of all things.
We too agree that the elements are a cause
   of whatever is formed from them,
so why bother giving it the name Ishvara?

118   *refuting a permanent cause, God*

The earth and other elements are not Ishvara,   119
for they are *multiple*, *impermanent*,
   without intention, and *not divine*.
They can be stepped on and are *impure*.

Space is not Ishvara either because it is inert.   120
Nor is he a permanent self
   for it has already been refuted.
And if the Creator is inconceivable,
   what is there to say of that which is beyond thought?

What is he supposed to create?   121
If he is a creator
   and the self, atoms, and so forth his creation,
this undermines your assertion of them as permanent.

As for a moment of consciousness,
we know it arises in dependence upon its object,
   not from Ishvara,
and that its continuum is beginningless.

Happiness and suffering are the results of   122
   virtuous and nonvirtuous actions, respectively.
So then, what did he create?

If the cause, a permanent God,
   is without beginning,

how could its effect,
   the creation of pleasure and pain,
   have a beginning?

If he does not depend on anything else,   123
   why does he not create continuously?
And since there is nothing whatsoever
   that is not created by him,
   on what would his productions depend?

If, on the other hand, creation depended on conditions,   124
the cause of the creation would be
   the accumulation of those conditions,
   not Ishvara.
In which case, if the conditions were accumulated,
   he would be unable not to create,
and if they were not,
   he would be unable to create.

If Ishvara were forced to create by other conditions,   125
he would be dominated by something else.
And if his actions were preceded by willful intention,
he would not be independent either
   but dependent upon his desires.
Thus the belief in an immutable God is repudiated.

The Vaishesika view that permanent atomic particles
   are the cause of the world
   was refuted above.

126   *refuting production from permanent atoms*

The Samkhyas assert a primal substance
   that is composed of the universal constituents:
   sattva, *rajas*, and *tamas* in equilibrium.
The unfolding universe is explained
   by their disequilibrium.

127   *refuting production from a permanent primal substance*

Yet how can a partless entity,
   namely the primal substance,
   have three natures?
And how can universal constituents truly exist,
for each one has three parts as well?

128

And if the universal constituents do not truly exist,
then the true existence of sound and so forth
   would be impossible.
How can pleasure, pain, or neutrality
be found in mindless things,
   such as the five sense objects?

129

If you argue that things have the nature of their causes,
have "things" not been analyzed?
For you, pleasure and the like are causes,
but from pleasure cloth has never sprung.

130

Even though pleasure and other feelings   131
may be due to things such as cloth,
when those causes are absent
pleasure is no more.
And the permanence of pleasure and so forth
　　has never been established.

If pleasure, for example, were permanent,   132
why is it not apprehended when there is pain?
If you say that it becomes subtle,
how can something that is permanent
　　be gross and then subtle?

It is subtle upon leaving its gross phase.   133
Its grossness and subtlety are impermanent.

Why then do you not accept everything to be
　　impermanent in the same way?
If pleasure fluctuates from grossness to subtlety,   134
it is obviously impermanent.

If you say that the effect does not exist
　　at the time of the cause,
then it could not arise.
It has to exist potentially before it manifests.

If the effect were present in the cause,   135
then eating food would be eating excrement.

And with the price of cloth,
one may as well buy cotton seeds and wear them.

You say that, due to their confusion,   136
    ordinary people do not see
    that the effect is present in the cause.
But that is the situation even for those
    who know reality.

Since you say that the knowledge   137
    that cause and effect have the same nature
    is also in ordinary people,
why don't they see it?
If you argue ordinary beings' perception is not valid,
then their perception of what is produced
    would also be false.

If valid cognition is not ultimately valid,   138
then indeed that which is known by it is also false.
In which case emptiness must also be false,
and therefore meditating on it is pointless.

Not having found the true existence   139
    that was falsely imputed by ignorance,
that absence of true existence is likewise
    not truly existent.
Therefore, when an existent thing is not found,
indeed its nonexistence is clearly not found as well.

When in a dream a son dies,   140
    the thought "He is dead"
    prevents the arising of
    the thought "He is alive."
However both thoughts are false
    since they are only dreams.

Therefore, after such analysis, it is seen that   141   *summary*
    nothing exists without a cause,
and nothing is found in either its single
    or combined causal conditions.

An effect is not present in its causes;   142
it is not inherently present
    upon having been produced;
and upon its cessation,
    it does not go anywhere else.
Objects do not exist in the way they appear;
in that sense they are like illusions.

Establishing conventional production
from causes

A magician's illusory creation   143   *reasoning from*
    and objects produced from causes   *dependent*
should be analyzed to realize how they come into being   *arising*
    and how they cease.

What is perceived only in conjunction 144
    with something else
    and not in its absence
is false, like a reflection in a mirror,
    and hence lacks true existence.

In the case of something that is nonexistent 145 *refuting inher-*
    or something that inherently exists, *ent production*
in either case, what need is there for a cause? *of existent and*
  nonexistent
  phenomena

A non-thing that does not exist 146
    will never be subject to change,
    even with millions of causes.
How can a non-thing
    ever become a thing?
And what else can become a thing? Nothing.

If at the time of being a non-thing, 147
    a thing does not exist,
how will it ever come into existence?
And that non-thing will never disappear
    as long as the existent thing is not produced.

As long as something is nonexistent, 148
it is impossible for its existence to emerge.
Nor can a truly existent entity,

which is permanent,
　　become nonexistent—
for these two can't coexist.

In this way, never is there any true arising   149
　　or true cessation,
and therefore this entire universe is devoid
　　of intrinsic production, duration, and cessation.

Upon analysis, states of existence are like dreams,   150
　　similar to plantain trees.
Ultimately, there is no difference between
　　those who have attained nirvana
　　and those who have not.

ENCOURAGEMENT TO REALIZE EMPTINESS

When all phenomena   151
　　are empty of inherent existence in this way,
what can be gained and what can be lost?
Who will be honored or despised by whom?

Where do happiness or suffering come from?   152
What is pleasant and what is unpleasant?
When analyzed, who is craving for what?

What is the world and who dies?   153
Who is a relative and who is a friend?

O you who are investigating reality,   154
please recognize, as I have,
    that everything is just like space!
Those wishing to be happy are
    greatly disturbed by conflict
    and overjoyed by pleasure.

Seeking happiness   155
    they commit many negative actions.
By arguing and hurting each other,
    they live in great hardship.

Even though they repeatedly come to happy existences   156
    and experience much pleasure,
upon dying they fall for a long time
    into the unbearable sufferings of lower realms.

In these abysses the apprehension   157
    of true existence
prevents the liberating comprehension
    of ultimate truth.

And if they do not realize ultimate truth,   158
they will continue to experience boundless suffering
where virtue is weak and lives are brief.

People strive to live long   159
   and avoid illness, hunger, and exhaustion.
Time is spent in sleep and meaningless activities.

Thus life passes quickly and in vain.   160
The opportunities to investigate reality are hard to find.
How then shall we reverse this beginningless habit
   of grasping at true existence?

Negative forces are exerting themselves   161
to cast us into unfortunate realms.
There, because of the abundance of wrong views,
faith in the right path is rare.

It will be hard to find the leisure of a human life again,   162
and harder still to come upon enlightened teachers.
This flood of disturbing emotions is difficult to forsake.
Sadly, sentient beings will continue to suffer!

O indeed it is worth feeling sorrow   163
   for those adrift in the river of pain
who, although they experience great misery,
   are unaware of their suffering.

For example, some ascetics suffer great hardship   164
by repeatedly exposing themselves to great heat
   or performing ablutions,
mistakenly believing they will reach liberation doing so.

Likewise, some think they have reached liberation,   165
    beyond the reach of aging and death,
yet experience great misery at death
    and in unfortunate rebirths.

When will I be able to extinguish the pains   166
    of those tormented by the fires of suffering
with the rain of my happiness
    sprung from the clouds of my virtues?

Respectfully accumulating merit and wisdom,   167
when will I be able to reveal emptiness
    to those who are suffering?

10
Dedication

By the virtues amassed through composing this work,   1
may all beings engage in the bodhisattva way of life.

May all those afflicted by physical and mental suffering   2
obtain oceans of happiness and contentment.
As long as they dwell in samsara,   3
   may their happiness never decline,
   and may they abide in the bliss of bodhisattvas.

May the hell beings enjoy the contentment   4   *for those*
   found in the Land of Bliss.   *suffering in*
   lower realms

May those afflicted with cold find warmth,   5
those oppressed by heat be cooled by rains
   pouring from the bodhisattvas' clouds of merit.
May the forest of sword-leaves become a pleasure grove   6
and the sword-like trees turn into wish-granting trees.

May the hells become vast pools of delight. 7
May the burning coals turn into jewels 8
and the mountains of crushing hells into celestial abodes.
May the rain of lava, coal, and daggers 9
    turn into a rain of flowers.
May those caught in the fiery river of acid, 10
    their flesh destroyed,
attain celestial bodies and dwell with gods and goddesses
    by peaceful streams.

Seeing the horrifying agents of Yama 11
    look up with fear at Vajrapani's shining form,
may beings' sins be purified.

Seeing a rain of lotuses and scented water 12
    extinguish the fires of hell,
may the beings there joyfully behold Avalokiteshvara.

May all beings be free of fear 13
and cheer upon seeing Manjushri. 14

Through my virtues, may those in hell find happiness 15
    upon seeing bodhisattvas headed by Samantabhadra,
and may their intense pain and fear be pacified.

May the animals be freed from fear 16
    of being preyed upon
and the hungry ghosts be satisfied by a stream of milk 17
    pouring from Avalokitesvara's hand.

May the blind see forms,   18   *for those*
   the deaf hear sounds,   *suffering in*
   and pregnant women give painless birth,   *upper realms*
   as did Mayadevi.
May beings acquire all they need: 19
   clothing, food, drink, and so forth.
May the fearful become fearless,   20
   those struck by grief find joy,
   the despondent become resolute,
   and the poor earn wealth.
May the ill regain good health   21
   and nobody ever get sick.
And may all beings be keen on helping each other.   22

May travelers find what they are looking for   23
and those traveling by boat   24
   safely reach shore
   and reunite with friends and relatives.
May those who travel in dangerous places   25
   find companions
   and be without fear and exhaustion.

May the deities protect the dull, the insane,   26
   the young, and the elderly.
May all attain a human state   27
   endowed with wisdom, faith, and love,
and may they remember their past lives.

Free of conflict or irritation,   28
  may they have inexhaustible wealth.
May beings of little splendor   29
  be endowed with magnificence,
the lowly come to excellence,   30
and the proud be humbled.

By this merit may all beings   31
  abstain from every vice
  and always engage in virtue.
May they engage in the bodhisattva way of life   32
  and always be cared for by the buddhas.

May all beings enjoy immeasurable lifespans,   33
  so even the word "death" disappears.
May the world be filled with wish-fulfilling trees,   34
  resounding with the sweetness of Dharma.
May the ground be free of stones,   35
  level like the palm of the hand,
  and smooth like lapis lazuli.

May bodhisattvas dwell everywhere,   36
adorning disciples with excellence.
May all beings uninterruptedly hear the Dharma   37
  from birds, trees, light, and even space itself.
May they meet buddhas and bodhisattvas,   38
  and may teachers be worshiped.

May rains be timely, harvests plentiful,   39
   people prosperous, and leaders be righteous.
May medicine be effective and mantras powerful,   40
   and may spirits be filled with compassion.

May no being ever suffer or commit evil.   41
May no one be afraid or depressed.

May monasteries flourish with scholarship   42
   and be harmonious.
May dedicated monastics find solitary places   43
   to meditate.
May their material needs be met   44
   and may they be unharmed.
May all ordained maintain pure ethics.
When discipline is broken,   45
   may they feel regret and purify,
   and thus obtain fortunate rebirths
   conducive for the practice of morality.

May the wise have abundance,   46
   pure minds,
   and widespread renown.
May beings never suffer in lower realms,   47
and may they gain enlightenment quickly.

May they revere the buddhas   48   *to higher aims*
and gain the inconceivable state of bliss.

May the bodhisattvas' and buddhas' wishes be fulfilled,   49
and may solitary realizers and hearers find happiness.   50

Through the kindness of Manjushri,   51   *for oneself*
    may I remember past lives
    and embrace monastic ordination in future ones.
May I always live sustained by simple food   52
    and find ideal solitude.
May Manjushri appear to me   53
    whenever I wish to see him or ask him something.
To satisfy the needs of infinite beings,   54
    may my way of life be just like his.

For as long as space endures,   55
    as long as beings remain,
until then may I too remain
    to ease the suffering of the world.

May all beings' suffering ripen upon me,   56
and may happiness be found
    through the virtues of bodhisattvas.

May the Dharma,   57   *for the*
    sole remedy of suffering   *teachings to*
    and source of all happiness,   *flourish*
    flourish forever.

I prostrate to Manjushri,
    whose kindness is the source of my virtue,
and to my spiritual teachers
    through whose inspiration I develop.

58   *homage*

Meditations

THERE IS A TREASURE of meditations that can be done based on Shantideva's *Bodhisattva Way of Life* or this abbreviated version. Here are just a few examples.

1. Prayers to soften the heart

In the Mahayana tradition, it is recommended to start one's meditation session by reciting and contemplating the seven limbs as a way to soften the heart. You can follow Shantideva's presentation of the seven limbs in the text.

- Start by taking refuge (2:26).
- Then begin the seven limbs with homage (2:23–25).
- Then make all the offerings or only some of them depending on time and the inspiration of the moment (2:2–22).
- Then, confession (2:27–65). The most complete purification is one that contains the four opponent powers. For the third power, the power of the antidotes, Shantideva mentions here following the All-Knowing Physician's advice, which means performing any virtuous action, like meditating on loving-kindness or emptiness. In 5:98, however, he advises us to recite the *Three Heaps Sutra* to cleanse the mind—so that could be done here as well.

◆ The remaining limbs of rejoicing, requesting teachings, asking the buddhas not to leave us, and dedication are found in chapter 3 in verses 1–22.

2. Taking the bodhisattva vow

As a Mahayana practitioner, we should remind ourselves daily of our determination to reach enlightenment rooted in our compassion for all beings.

The elaborate way to do so would be to start with Meditation 1, then recite the verses on taking the bodhisattva vows three times (3:23–24), and finally rejoice in the good deed just done (3:25–34).

A shorter way would be to just take refuge (2:26), then as above take the vows three times (3:23–24) and rejoice in the good deed just done (3:25–34).

3. The benefits of bodhichitta

Bodhichitta is the most awakened state of mind you can induce, and it has so many good qualities. To contemplate bodhichitta, start by reading 1:4–6. Stop there and think about it. Then recite some of the verses 1:7–36. Find one that speaks to your heart and infuse your mind with its meaning.

4. A warm altruistic state of mind

Reflect often and deeply on the fact that we living beings are all equal in wanting happiness and that to care vastly for others is what brings about inner joy. Read and contemplate 8:90–112.

5. Downside of selfishness and benefits of altruism

Even though we may have already generated the aspiration to be good, there can be inertia, due to habits cultivated over a long time, that naturally makes us return to our selfish ways. To counteract this we have to reflect often on the downside of selfishness and the benefits of altruism. Read and contemplate 8:113–139.

6. Healthy and unhealthy ways to compare ourselves with others

In our relationships we compare ourselves with others, and that is natural. In some instances we may realize that we possess certain qualities of learning or whatever that others don't. To feel happy and rejoice about this is fine, but to feel superior and arrogant would be inappropriate. Likewise, when we see positive qualities in others, to develop the wish to gain those same qualities is excellent. Generating envy or jealousy, however, just makes us miserable. Healthy competition is useful in the sense that it inspires us to do our best. However, if we lose respect for others, then we have gone wrong. Read and contemplate 8:140–158.

7. Giving and taking

To make our heart warm and peaceful and to create a state of mind that wishes to benefit others through our thoughts and actions, the mental exercise of giving with love while exhaling and taking with compassion while inhaling is very effective. Before using your own life's experiences, reading 8:159–173 can put you in the right state of mind.

8. Two levels of reality

In the Madhyamaka approach to how things exist, there is a presentation of the two truths. Ordinary beings see everything as self-existent, and based on that, mental afflictions such as inflated attachment or aversion arise in their minds. Under their influence they act impulsively, thereby creating the cause for rebirth in an unenlightened world.

Advanced meditators, however, see everything as being empty of this self-existence. Expressed in another way, they see things as being merely designated by the mind on a collection of causes and parts, which themselves are also merely designated, and so on ad infinitum. Such a view, which accords with how things actually exist, gradually frees these meditators from compulsive rebirth, leaving them free to take birth where it is of most benefit (9:1–14 and 30–40).

9. Is everything mind-stuff or empty of self-existence?

If you are in the mood to stretch your mind, you could reflect on various possibilities of how the world exists and what realizations are needed to achieve eternal happiness.

In chapter 9, Shantideva creates an imaginary debate with proponents of various views existing at that time in India, himself upholding the subtlest Buddhist view, that of the Madhyamaka.

Buddha taught different levels of realization required for individuals to reach liberation, in accordance with the level of intelligence of his listeners. One view, that of the Chittamatra, or Mind Only, school, says that the world is mind-stuff or that subject and object are mind and that this mind is self-existent. The Madhyamaka view is the one that Shantideva defends in this debate (9:15–29).

10. How do I really exist?

Our misapprehension of the I is the cause of the mental afflictions that generate all our problems. Shantideva doesn't say that the I doesn't exist at all but simply that it is not findable. Therefore it exists as a mere designation. But it *does* exist and can even reach the state of omniscience with the ability to help all beings.

If we observe carefully our sense of I, we start noticing that "I" sometimes refers to our body, sometimes to our mind, sometimes to both together. If we are not satisfied with this vagueness and investigate minutely, we won't find the I where we thought it was and are left with an absence, an empty space. The I doesn't exist in this self-existent, findable way. But it obviously does exist, so how? In a relative way, the I exists as something very nebulous, as a mere designation on the body-mind complex (9:56–77).

11. How do phenomena really exist?

If we don't look too closely, everything that exists seems to actually be there, on the base of what we point at. For example, the body is there sitting on the chair. But if we start investigating, where exactly is the body? Is it found in any of its parts, or in the collection of its parts? When we inquire in this way, something happens to the mind. The body we thought was so obviously there is not found by the mind, and we are left with a question mark. If we don't find it there, then how does it exist? After investigating further we come to the conclusion that it exists as a mere designation. Likewise, when we investigate the parts of the body and so on down to their atoms, or other things such as our feelings or our mind, they all seem to be there until examined more closely. Isn't that perplexing? In each session, read just a few verses and reflect on their meaning (9:78–115).

12. Encouragement to realize how things exist

Sometimes we forget the importance of inquiring exactly how things exist, so reading these verses revives our curiosity.

- ◆ On the benefits of realizing emptiness (9:52–55)
- ◆ For encouragement to realize emptiness (9:151–167)

13. Remembering that life is precious

It is easy to take life for granted, subconsciously thinking we have plenty of time and that someday we will train wholeheartedly. But time misused can never be regained, so it is important to often read reminders of the preciousness of our human life, even as a daily morning motivation (4:13–48 and 1:4–6).

14. Cultivating mindfulness to gently tame the mind
How fast we make progress on our way to inner peace depends on our ability to be mindful moment by moment. These verses are a friendly reminder of the importance of mindfulness and how to cultivate it. It's better to read only a paragraph at a time and use it as a mirror to investigate your own behavior (5:1–109).

15. Dealing with anger
In life we often get irritable or upset when facing adverse circumstances or dealing with difficult people. This state of mind is unpleasant both for ourselves and for those around us. And if we don't apply antidotes to this bad mood, it can have disagreeable consequences. It can lead to depression or social isolation, and even those closest to us can suffer from our volatile behavior. Shantideva dedicates a whole chapter to exploring ways to overcome and prevent anger. By the end of the chapter he is even able to convince us that problems are helpful and indispensable to our inner growth!

Here again, it's better to read a few verses at a time, stopping at an argument that catches your attention, and seeing how you could apply it to your life (6:1–134).

16. Me, lazy? Procrastinating? Nooo! Mmm...
If this title corresponds to your present state of mind, you may find it invigorating to read 7:1–15.

17. Feeling low or lacking enthusiasm
When feeling discouraged or lacking in energy, it may be helpful to read Shantideva's explanation of how to cheer yourself up and set the best pace for your inner adventure. He explains here how to generate aspiration, self-confidence, and joy, and he even advises us to rest (7:16–76).

18. Generating positive thoughts

If you are feeling selfish or haven't had a good day, reading part of Shantideva's dedication will help change your mood. It is an especially good read before going to sleep, to ensure that our rest is peaceful and virtuous (10:1–58).

About the Author

Venerable René Feusi trained as a florist for the purpose of taking over the family business of flower shops in Geneva, Switzerland. In 1979, while on a spiritual quest in India and Nepal, he met Lama Yeshe and Lama Zopa Rinpoche, who were to become his main teachers, at the month-long November course at Kopan Monastery in Kathmandu Valley. Until his ordination he would spend half the year working in the family business and the other half receiving teachings and doing retreats.

At the advice of Lama Zopa Rinpoche in 1985, he took ordination as a novice monk from Losang Nyingma Rinpoche, abbot of Namgyal Monastery, and then a year later full ordination from His Holiness the Dalai Lama. He spent two more years in India and Nepal receiving teachings and doing retreats before joining Nalanda Monastery in the south of France. Khensur Rinpoche Geshe Tekchog was the abbot and teacher at that time. In his four years there, he studied a number of texts on the graduated path to enlightenment, mind training, as well as various philosophical texts.

After completing the traditional nine preliminary practices, he entered a two-and-a-half-year solitary retreat at Oseling Centro de Retiro in Spain. Since completing that, he has spent half his time teaching and leading retreats at Dharma centers largely in Europe and the United States, including being resident teacher at Vajrapani Institute in California from 2001 to 2007. The other half of his time is spent in retreat.

About Wisdom Publications

WISDOM PUBLICATIONS is the leading publisher of classic and contemporary Buddhist books and practical works on mindfulness. Publishing books from all major Buddhist traditions, Wisdom is a nonprofit charitable organization dedicated to cultivating Buddhist voices the world over, advancing critical scholarship, and preserving and sharing Buddhist literary culture.

To learn more about us or to explore our other books, please visit our website at www.wisdompubs.org. You can subscribe to our eNewsletter, request a print catalog, and find out how you can help support Wisdom's mission either online or by writing to:

Wisdom Publications
199 Elm Street
Somerville, Massachusetts 02144 USA

You can also contact us at 617-776-7416 or info@wisdompubs.org.

Wisdom is a 501(c)(3) organization, and donations in support of our mission are tax deductible.

Wisdom Publications is affiliated with the Foundation for the Preservation of the Mahayana Tradition (FPMT).

More Books from Wisdom Publications

ENLIGHTENMENT TO GO
Shantideva and the Power of Compassion to Transform Your Life
288 pages, $17.95, ebook $13.08

One of *Spirituality and Practice*'s Best Spiritual Books of 2011.

BECOMING THE COMPASSION BUDDHA
Tantric Mahamudra for Everyday Life
Lama Thubten Yeshe
Edited by Robina Courtin
Foreword by Geshe Lhundub Sopa
224 pages, $14.95, ebook $10.89

"Lama Yeshe expresses the profundity of Buddha's teachings in a clear, pene-
trating, yet easily accessible way that enables us to see ourselves and our Buddha
potential. Through his instructions on *The Inseparability of the Spiritual Master
and Avalokiteshvara*, we gain the confidence and skill to overcome our 'poor
quality' self-image and transform ourselves into the Compassion Buddha."
—Thubten Chodron, coauthor of *Buddhism: One Teacher, Many Traditions*

VAST AS THE HEAVENS, DEEP AS THE SEA
Verses in Praise of Bodhicitta
Khunu Rinpoche, Gareth Sparham
Foreword by His Holiness the Dalai Lama
160 pages, $16.95, ebook $12.35

"Khunu Rinpoche, through his loving presence and great kindness, was one of the most profound influences on me in India in the early 1970s. This book is a wonderful, inspiring evocation of him, and of the path of lovingkindness." —Sharon Salzberg, author of *Lovingkindness: The Revolutionary Art of Happiness*

TO DISPEL THE MISERY OF THE WORLD
Whispered Teachings of the Bodhisattvas
224 pages, $16.95, ebook $12.35
Ga Rabjampa
Foreword by Khenpo Appey
Translated by Rigpa Translations

"For anyone yearning to lead a more sane and altruistic life in these troubling times, the practice of lojong, or 'training the mind' in compassion, is a simply priceless tool."—Sogyal Rinpoche, author of *The Tibetan Book of Living and Dying*

THE AWAKENING MIND
The Foundation of Buddhist Thought, Volume 4
Geshe Tashi Tsering
Foreword by Lama Zopa Rinpoche
192 pages, $14.95, ebook $10.89

"A simple and systematic introduction to Buddhist philosophy and practice." —*Eastern Horizon*